Hatfield Poly

Hatfield Campus
College Lane. ...d
Herts A 10 Campus
Ball Park, **Hertford**
... OF

...wed
...elow.

PRACTICAL SOCIAL WORK

Series Editor: Jo Campling

(BASW)

Social work is at an important stage in its development. All professions must be responsive to changing social and economic conditions if they are to meet the needs of those they serve. This series focuses on sound practice and the specific contribution which social workers can make to the well-being of our society.

The British Association of Social Workers has always been conscious of its role in setting guidelines for practice and in seeking to raise professional standards. The conception of the Practical Social Work series arose from a survey of BASW members to discover where they, the practitioners in social work, felt there was the most need for new literature. The response was overwhelming and enthusiastic, and the result is a carefully planned, coherent series of books. The emphasis is firmly on practice, set in a theoretical framework. The books will inform, stimulate and promote discussion, thus adding to the further development of skills and high professional standards. All the authors are practitioners and teachers of social work representing a wide variety of experience.

JO CAMPLING

PRACTICAL SOCIAL WORK

Series Editor: Jo Campling

(BASW)

Anti-Racist Social Work

A Challenge for White Practitioners and Educators

Lena Dominelli

Foreword by John Small

M

MACMILLAN
EDUCATION

First published 1988

Published by
MACMILLAN EDUCATION LTD
Houndmills, Basingstoke, Hampshire RG21 2XS
and London
Companies and representatives
throughout the world

Typeset by TecSet Ltd, Wallington, Surrey

Printed in Hong Kong

British Library Cataloguing in Publication Data
Dominelli, Lena
Anti-racist social work: a challenge for
white practitioners and educators
1. Social service and race relations
— Great Britain
I. Title
361.32   HV245
ISBN 0–333–30906–5 (hardcover)
ISBN 0–333–30907–3 (paperback)

Contents

Foreword

Institutionalised oppression is a major force operating in
Britain today. As a part of this process racism is the
fundamental barrier preventing access to opportunity, privilege, power and social justice for the black population. It is
against this background that this book is written. It is
designed to bring to the foreground the effect of racism in
social work education and training and to demonstrate how
the various elements of racist practice are stitched into the
fabric of social work. It has been said that the teacher today
is teaching what has been learned at least two generations
ago from textbooks that were written several decades
before. In the area of social work this is certainly the case,
and in relation to social work with black people the problem
is multiplied in that social work theoreticians have largely
ignored the presence of the black population, and so in their
theory-building no attention has been paid to the effects of
racism on the black population. The immediate and central
task must therefore be to reorientate the value base of
social work in a real way to confront racism in its various
forms. This book recognises the urgency of doing this.
Without work of this nature, stereotyping and the reinforcing
of racist practices is likely to continue without being challenged. The first task is to acknowledge differences and
identify similarities, but the danger of course is that often
differences become generalised into stereotypes, and this we
must constantly guard against. Lena Dominelli's work has
demonstrated that generalisation performs an important
function in terms of making sense of new situations.
However, as she has shown, generalisation should not be a
substitute for accurate description of new situations, of
observation, analysis and logical deduction based on the

level of current knowledge. This book demonstrates how the process of generalisation can be transformed into stereotyping and then feed into the structure of racism.

Lena Dominelli is writing to contribute to positive action in the area of anti-racist practice to contextualise the black experience and white reaction and to contribute to current dialogue with those who are becoming increasingly aware and concerned about the extent and effect of racism. Its existence is not only in the network of our institutions but also in our students as they pass through the teaching institutions, as actors in society, and in their interaction with their black clients. The book appropriately begins with identifying the nature of racism and need for anti-racist training in which the context of the subject is clarified, and anchored within the real world, thereby suggesting that the white population must take positive action to eradicate as far as possible racism and then go on to show the ways in which racism permeates all aspects of society, thereby becoming a common concern for the theoretician and the professional alike.

The book shows how important the issue of racism is for the practice of social work with black people. It suggests that if social workers do not understand the dynamics of racism then they cannot deliver effective services to black communities since the experience of black people in Britain is being constantly shaped by racism. Lena Dominelli cautions us against conceiving the experience of black people as one lodged exclusively within the context of class, thereby conveniently avoiding the necessity to define, to analyse and to take action that enables social workers to become much more aware of the nature and effect of racism within the social work profession. Her work suggests that contemporary social work has given the *impression* that it has taken on board issues to do with class, gender, racism and ethnicity. However, this is *not* the case. In the process of imparting knowledge and in the application of social work principles, racism and the subjective experience of the black population in Britain are largely ignored. Consequently, the profession has maintained a pathological view of black families based on conceptualisations anchored in racism and transmitted through concepts of deprivation and maladaption to the existing social order. This is no doubt true to the tradition, framework and elements which govern the relationship between the colonialised and the colonialiser.

In this book, however, the power relationship between the black client and the white worker is brought out in a way which gives a glimpse into the dynamics of social relationships between the races in an oppressive and racist society and also the intricacies and the part played by bureaucratic structures as they operate within teaching institutions and social work agencies. In this regard the expertise of the black worker is seen as rooted in the knowledge and experience of the black community and so gives the black worker a special authority which threatens the white bureaucracy, whose authority is based not on the knowledge and experience of black people but on the authority of office rather than the authority of expertise.

Lena Dominelli has not fallen into the trap of suggesting that social work can transform society or that the sole responsibility for anti-racist practices lies with social workers. Far from it; she has recognised that 'there is much that the state can do which is not only consistent with liberty, but is essential to it'.

Power is conceived within the context of social relationships. Therefore, the central concern must be with the process and phenomenon of institutionalisation which perpetuates certain social patterns and make them endure over time, and therefore outlast the individual, thereby transmitting behaviour and attitudes from one generation to the next. This work has indicated very clearly that our lives are affected by our face-to-face interpersonal relationships, and therefore the eradication of racism should necessarily increase the quality of life for both the black and white population.

Social work practice involves the use of knowledge from a variety of traditions and disciplines, and so there are conflicting approaches and conflicting evidence. However, it is becoming increasingly clear that because of the nature of racism and ways in which it is embedded in the various traditions there must necessarily be a radical anti-racist approach to it. Society has accepted the responsibility to educate and train social workers. Therefore society must accept the responsibility of taking affirmative action to eradicate racism.

The book also describes the experience of the black population in Britain in terms of the entrenchment of racism not only in the national but in the local states. It emphasises the relationship between the development of racism both in its historical and contemporary context, and explains the processes whereby the black population is relegated to the lower strata of society and at one and the same time it shows how the colour-blind and pathological view is brought to the understanding of the needs of the black population. For example, Lena Dominelli has given us a view as to how the pathology of the black family has developed among white practitioners and converged with white sexism which is then played out among professionals and between the white professional and the black client alike. In order to create a profound shift Lena Dominelli has addressed the issue of positive action by tackling racism within the context of the organisation; and so has called for an anti-racist strategy. But by what means can this be brought about? Lena Dominelli's proposal is to bring about the transformation of social work through the development of equal opportunities policy anchored in an anti-racist framework, followed by fair recruitment and selection processes, combined with training which attacks the values and norms of the organisation, together with checks and balances to monitor the process of implementation with appropriate feed-back mechanisms to reflect a clear anti-racist path. Lena Dominelli sees a central role for managers both at the senior-management and middle-management level, since any manager who manages others has a significant and supporting role in terms of implementing policy and ensuring that subordinates do not act in a discriminatory or racist manner. To this end it is made clear that at the outset key managers must necessarily undergo anti-racism-awareness training to become sensitive to how their own attitudes can perpetuate racism. Anti-racism awareness training should be related to the impact of discriminatory practice on day-to-day decision-making processes of higher- and lower-level managers alike, resulting in managers and indeed practitioners developing the requisite skills and appropriate attitudes in relation to the black population.

Lena Dominelli is pessimistic in view of the fact that, irrespective of the increasing concern about racism in this society and its impact on blacks and whites alike, teaching institutions and social services and voluntary agencies have turned a blind eye to the issue of racism. The major challenge of social work must therefore be the removal of racism – to constitute the starting-point for the reconceptualisation of social work in a multi-racial society. It must be recognised that racism permeates all aspects of society and therefore educational institutions and social welfare agencies are affected similarly. Consequently, for Lena Dominelli, the effect of racism on social work practice should be obvious. The greater part of the problem which is currently being experienced by black people, she suggests, is engendered by the underlying structure of racism and therefore any attempt to alleviate this problem from the traditional casework basis is doomed to fail. It should therefore be clear that what is required is a radical rethinking and recasting of social work programmes based on an anti-racist strategy. The field of social work with black people is composed of contradictory philosophies, moderate thought and racist assumptions. Indeed, social work has been a moving frontier of confusion, particiularly when it attempts to move across race and cultures. Lena Dominelli has shown that the social work approach has moved from grand concepts of assimilation, integration, adaptation (and colour equal problems), to cultural explanations which currently leave the profession unwilling to challenge, and uncertain about challenging, racism. But because this book goes beyond these it will meet the needs of social work practitioners and educators alike. It will prove to be an invaluable source for teachers, social workers, community workers, and people who are interested in the nature of racism and its effect on the black and white population and the process whereby measures can be taken to remove this destructive phenomenon from the profession in particular and society in general. It will undoubtedly be a source of practical assistance to those who are concerned with the creation of a truly multi-racial society.

JOHN SMALL
Assistant Director
London Borough of Hackney Social Services Department

Acknowledgements

Black people and their struggles to assert their humanity and dignity in a racist world have been crucial in inspiring the reclamation of my own humanity following the experiences of being a non-patrial immigrant in several continents. The lessons I have drawn from these have influenced my thinking as well as my practice and are reflected in my approach to the question of eliminating racism. The insights I have gained from these experiences have led me to feel passionately that racism is more than evil, irrational prejudices held by individuals. It is also a powerful social force which operates coherently and systematically to invade and structure every human interaction. I want to thank my many friends, black and white, who have helped in the writing of this book by making me think deeply of who I was and what I am. I also wish to express my gratitude to the many generations of Warwick students and practice teachers who have influenced my thinking about the subject and who have taught me a great deal, as did the clients and workers, black and white, who agreed to be interviewed by me in connection with this book. I should add that the material contained in the case studies has been altered to protect the identity of the individuals concerned. Finally, I wish to thank the readers of the text who have provided me with encouragement and comments which have enabled me to maintain my arguments in an emotionally fraught and complex area. In particular, I would like to thank Paul Stubbs and Martin Willis. I also extend very special thanks to John Small for finding time in his busy schedule to write the foreword.

LENA DOMINELLI

In honour of the struggles of little girls who long for blonde hair and blue eyes, but learn after much hardship and pain to be proud of their own attributes

Introduction:
Anti-Racist Social Work – A
Critical Issue for White People

The British population consists of people with diverse national origins, different cultural backgrounds and economic positions. Yet white social workers have not come to grips with the ethnically pluralistic nature of British society nor have they reflected this in their practice by making available services which cater for the specific needs and demands of ethnic minorities (ADSS/CRE, 1979). Their failure to do so has made countering racism a most pressing issue in social work education, training and practice. Working out how to respond to this task is both difficult and controversial. The paths whereby the elimination of racism is achieved are fraught with minefields. That there are no easy answers lying readily to hand is amply revealed when we examine the history and outcome of our recent struggles against racism. The definitions of what it is 'appropriate' to do have varied significantly as our understanding of the nature of the forces we have been opposing has deepened. What seemed permissible yesterday is being exposed as suspect today, and looks like being even more questionable tomorrow. White liberals desperately seeking to do the 'right thing' by black people have found it increasingly difficult to define their present position, let alone their next action, as all they stand for becomes discredited through racism awareness training and as their activities aimed at combating racism are revealed as either inadequate or positively damaging to black people when evaluated through a black perspective.

From a black perspective, white people's attempts to make black people feel welcome in Britain by assimilating them into the (white) 'British way of life' have been found wanting for being based on arrogant assumptions that white people and white culture have something to offer black people, whilst black people and their culture provide nothing in return (Gilroy, 1987). The assimilationist position has rendered black people's day-to-day experience of racism invisible, ignored the positive contributions they have made and are making to society, and denied their resistance to oppression. White people's efforts in overcoming the weaknesses of the assimilationist approach have led to the development of an 'ethnically sensitive' perspective which at least recognises some of the cultural strengths of black people's life-styles and their contributions to society. However, this too has been quickly downgraded as a diversionary activity focusing attention on black people and their communities rather than on white people and their power structures, thereby blaming those at the receiving end of racism instead of the social relations creating it (Gilroy, 1987). The attempt to refine the 'ethnically sensitive' approach through 'multi-culturalism' and 'multi-racialism' as the embodiments of equality between different races and different cultures has also been found wide of the mark. Racial inequality has not disappeared because white people understand better the customs, traditions and religious activities of ethnic minority groups. And the racial harmony which both black and white people have sought has proved singularly elusive outside the atmosphere of shared social festivities (Ohri and Manning, 1982).

Although our efforts at eliminating racism have so far been ineffective, many white people are still searching for solutions. Those of us struggling against racism from an anti-racist perspective are quite clear that whatever we do, we must tackle racism at its core by combining change at the personal level with organisational change. Anti-racist approaches to countering racism have attracted those of us wishing to transcend the limitations inherent in the other approaches open to white people. I take the view that white people cannot have a black perspective because that is based on the experience of being black in a white racist society and challenging racism from that position. However, I do believe that white people can, nay must, be anti-racist.

I feel it is appropriate for me, as a white person writing this book from an anti-racist perspective, to address white people interested in anti-racist social work and to share the experiences gained from attempting to implement anti-racist practices in both my personal and my professional life. Although my main audience will be white social work educators and practitioners, for I cannot and would not speak for black people, I acknowledge that the things I say carry implications for black people, whether it be exhorting white people to become involved in the anti-racist struggle or demanding the establishment of egalitarian relations between black and white people as a precondition for our working together.

Anti-racist perspectives focus on transforming the unequal social relations shaping social interaction between black and white people into egalitarian ones. Additionally, these offer white people hope – hope of changing society in egalitarian directions. In being committed to making racial equality a reality, white people working from an anti-racist perspective can build bridges between themselves and black people working towards the same objective from a black perspective.

Until recently, white social workers have adopted the view that racism is a societal problem requiring government intervention, rather than being a central concern of theirs as either practitioners or trainers (ADSS/CRE, 1978). Fortunately this attitude is shifting. It is doing so whilst social work is both in a state of flux and under attack. Pressure for change is emanating from privatisation measures; managerial imperatives aimed at improving efficiency and coping with a situation of dwindling resources; legislative requirements, particularly in relation to child care, mental health and social security; increasing public scrutiny of social work, especially in the area of child abuse; consumer demands for more sensitive, unstigmatised and less oppressive services;

and social workers' own emerging activism as they organise collectively to defend their rights as workers and the services they provide.

Meanwhile social work has been found wanting by critics from a variety of perspectives. The 'New Right' castigates it for its 'do-gooding' propensities and its failure in controlling people and ensuring their conformity to 'acceptable', i.e. white middle class heterosexual standards of behaviour (Minford, 1984; Gilder, 1982). The white Left criticises it for being primarily about control (Bailey and Brake, 1975; Bolger *et al.*, 1981; Simpkins, 1980). White feminists take it to task for its sexist theories and practices (Brook and Davis, 1985; Wilson, 1977; Statham, 1978; Dominelli, 1986; Marchant and Wearing, 1986). Black women and men condemn it for its pervasive racism (ABSWAP, 1981; Devine, 1983; Small, 1987; Manning and Ohri, 1982). Facing attack on all fronts and the rupturing of established routines and assumptions about their place in the world, white people in social work teaching and practice have felt confused, de-skilled, and uncertain about the direction they should now take.

White fears and anxieties about the process of becoming anti-racist rise to the fore. White professionals worry about making social work a 'political' subject, feel guilty about colluding with racism and seem powerless in the enormous task of struggling against it. They are concerned about the price they will have to pay, given their current unprepared-ness and lack of skills, which might result in their losing out in the employment stakes.

White people have difficulty accepting their exclusion from activities which black people have redefined as theirs, e.g. working with black families (Stubbs, 1985), or teaching black students. Such exclusion is problematic because white people are not used to having their power challenged by black people in this way. They resent having discrete areas of *their* social order defined 'out of bounds' by those whom they 'rule'; whose place in society they have designated as inferior; and whose activities they have sought to control. White people experience anger because the normal power relationship between them and black people has been unilaterally ruptured. Moreover, white people consider their intervention in black people's lives beneficial. To be told that they have no right to interfere in black people's lives in the pernicious ways to which they have grown accustomed comes as a shock to well-meaning whites. As does black people's directive that white people's priority should be to sort themselves, not black people, out. Encouraging white people to participate actively in the establishment of anti-racist social work is problematic. White people feeling tainted by the pervasiveness of racism in British society find the prospect of becoming involved in eradicating racism so daunting that they are tempted to ignore it altogether. Others are so consumed by guilt that they feel incapable of acting even though they are extremely worried about the continuation of racist practices (Powell and Edmonds, 1985).

White people wonder how they can best respond to these criticisms whilst recognising the constraints of being state employees with legal statutory requirements to fulfil. Desperately seeking to resolve the tension between care and control in their work, they discover developing non-oppressive forms of practice in general, and anti-racist and anti-sexist practice in particular, complex and difficult. Without wanting to suggest there are easy solutions, I would argue that we need not feel so helpless in the face of the challenge before us. Our feelings of powerlessness and inability to change things can be countered if white social work educators and practitioners accept the importance of struggling against racism and take up the issue of transforming social work education and practice in directions which promote people's welfare and empower welfare users. An anti-racist perspective in social work provides one avenue whereby such changes can be achieved.

The anti-racist perspective may seem harsh in its judgments of many of our well-intentioned activities and motives. But this is unavoidable when the measure of our endeavours is not what we think of them, but the extent to which our efforts actually dismantle racism. We can make considerable progress in anti-racist directions if we are sufficiently motivated in wanting to change our world and organise collectively in order to achieve this. This book aims to help us in this task by providing an analysis which evaluates critically those practices which we consider indicative of 'successful' or racism-free social work and by suggesting principles on which future action leading to the establishment of anti-racist social work might be based.

What is racism?

Racism, the scourge pervading every aspect of social interaction, is 'the belief in the inherent superiority of one race over all others and thereby the right to dominance' (Lorde, 1984, p.115). Explaining racism by trying to define the complex social relations it encompasses is tricky. The very language we use is riddled with racism. When white people, including social work educators and practitioners speak of Britain, they usually mean white, 'English' Britain. Becoming aware of the implicit racism in the word makes white anti-racists hesistant in using it. But, as yet, we have neither reclaimed the word by divesting it of the racist ideologies and practices embedded within it, nor have we developed an appropriate alternative to it. 'Multi-racial Britain' does not meet anti-racist criteria because racism penetrates more than the cultural dimension of human organisation. 'Multi-racialism' has become a concept through which white people obscure the real problem that needs to be tackled – racism – and focus instead on discovering one another's different lifestyles, almost as if cultural interactions between black and white people were independent of structurally reproduced and reinforced inequality (CCCS, 1982).

British racism is about the construction of social relationships on the basis of an assumed inferiority of non-Anglo-Saxon ethnic minority groups and flowing from this, their exploitation and oppression. Racism is apparent in the minutiae of everyday life as well as institutions and legislation and permeates every aspect of our personal and professional lives whether we are black or white, making confronting it difficult and complex. I use the term 'non-Anglo-Saxon ethnic minorities' to include all those people, black and white, who are not considered 'indigenous' British of white English and Nordic European origins, settled in Britain. The 1981 Census revealed that 4 per cent of the British populace is of 'New Commonwealth' or black origins. Other significant ethnic minority groups include the Chinese, Greek Cypriots, Jews, Poles, Italians and Irish. These groups constitute the non-Anglo-Saxon ethnic minorities found in British society, making racism more than a matter of black and white. Although there are significant sub-divisions within this categorisation, each of which justifies being written about in its own right, the discourse in this book is conducted largely in terms of black and white. I do this because the groups currently being subjected to the most vicious and intractable expressions of racism in Britain are black people, i.e. those of Asian, African and Caribbean descent (CCCS, 1982; Bryan, 1985; Smith, 1976; Brown, 1984). I focus on this division because the racism being perpetrated against black people is such a fundamental and integral part of society that eradicating the racism white people level against them will also provide the solution in countering the racism experienced by other non-Anglo-Saxon ethnic minority groups.

Operating on a hierarchical continuum placing Anglo-Saxon Britons at the superior end of the spectrum and Asian and Afro-Caribbean Britons at its corresponding inferior point, racism politicises race and ethnicity through relations of domination and subordination. The politicisation of human biology in white supremacist terms has enabled white people at the top of this racialised hierarchy to construct social relations imposing their definitions of the world over others, thereby maintaining their privileges and power. From the standpoint of those endorsing the biological determinism of racial inferiority, each person is endowed at birth with immutable characteristics based on white superiority and black inferiority (Jensen, 1971; Eysenck, 1972; Gobineau, 1953). Social organisation based on white supremacist terms has been perpetuated as a 'natural' state of affairs over which people have no control. Concentrating on the biological aspects of racism mystifies the social nature of the relationships embedded in racist practices and facilitates the scapegoating and instant oppression of those having easily visible racial and ethnic characteristics, e.g. skin colour, hair type, language and cultural traditions. The politicisation of these characteristics indicates that racism goes beyond biological characteristics and is socially constructed. This dimension of racism has been acknowledged by some local authorities in their policy formulation. The London Borough of Lambeth, for example, has incorporated the social construction of racism in its definition of 'black' in its child care policy document. It says: '*Black*'. A description of any person whose skin colour renders them liable to the application of racism, irrespective of ethnic background, linguistic or academic ability, country of origin, or length of stay' (Lambeth, SS 208/80–81).

Clarifying the social construction of racism, Stuart Hall defines racism as a set of economic, political and ideological practices through which a dominant group exercises hegemony over subordinate groups (Hall, 1980, p.338). Establishing hegemony or dominance means that the ruling group must capture people's hearts and minds in a common-sensical, seemingly untheorised way which secures their consent to being dominated without being conscious of it. The unarticulated nature of racism makes it difficult for the majority of white people to see racism as an endemic feature of society, permeating all aspects of it. It also enables white people to perceive racism as the crude, irrational beliefs and actions manifest by a few National Front supporters instead of a normal feature of social interaction between black and white and acquire a self-concept which is not racist. Hence, white people generally take exceptional umbrage at being called racist. The Labour Party leadership's reaction to Sharon Atkin calling the Labour Party racist (*Guardian*, 30 April 1987) exemplifies this. During this incident, the electorate of Nottingham East had Mohammed Aslam imposed upon them as their prospective Labour candidate in place of Sharon Atkin. Labour leaders nullified her candidature when she branded the Labour Party racist for its refusal to endorse autonomous Black Sections within it.

Racism consists of three main elements interacting with one another: *individual racism, institutional racism,* and *cultural racism* (Bromley, 1972). Individual racism is made up of those attitudes and behaviours depicting a negative prejudgment of racial groups. Individual racist attitudes without institutional backing constitute racial prejudice. Institutional racism consists of customary routines which ration resources and power by excluding racially inferior groups. Relying on public power and authority for its legitimation, institutionalised racism pathologises these excluded groups for their lack of success within the system and blames them for their predicament. The reproduction of racism through the interaction between individual behaviour and institutional norms forms the dynamics of institutionalised racism. Cultural racism is centred around those values, beliefs and ideas endorsing the superiority of white culture. It provides the cement of popular racism which reinforces both institutional and individual racism. The impact of cultural, institutionalised and individual racism is felt by all non-Anglo-Saxon ethnic minority groups.

Being centred on social relations asserting the supremacy of white Anglo-Saxon British, and ensuring these are accepted as 'commonsense', racism provides the ideological coherence necessary for the white Anglo-Saxon British to maintain their position, deny non-Anglo-Saxon minority ethnic groups access to social power and resources, and trample on their racial integrity and dignity. 'Commonsense' forms the basis of the 'new racism' (Barker, 1981) currently featuring in Britain's political and social life.

The 'new racism' has developed as the white Anglo-Saxon British response to Britain's declining socio-economic position and the existence of a substantial, settled, indigenous black population. Through it, white British nationhood is being redefined. The 'new racism' has acquired legal force through the concepts of nationality and citizenship embodied in the 1981 Nationality Act and made 'repatriation' a respectable option for those denied British citizenship – mainly black 'non-patrials'. This new concept of nationhood excludes the Black British whose culture the 'new racists' see as '*different from*', i.e. inferior to, that of the white indigenous population. Because what is at stake revolves around those whose culture is deemed insignificant and whose human status is diminished in consequence, the 'new racism' legitimates the continued exploitation and harassment of black people.

Barker (1981, p.18) contends that the 'new racism' is not based on white people claiming superior status. However, I challenge his assertion on the grounds that the new construction of racism has pushed underground overt statements of white Anglo-Saxon British supremacy. By affirming the Anglo-Saxon 'British way of life' because it is 'different' from other people's who are also entitled to defend their own way of life – in their own countries, the 'new racists' elevate the white Anglo-Saxon British way of life above all others, thereby speaking from an anglocentric perspective rather than one positing equality and the possibility of co-existence between different ways of life. The black British way of life is specifically avoided as an 'alien' pollutant in their 'sacred' environment (Cohen, 1985). In describing the black British way of life thus, it is clear the 'new racists' consider it inferior to the white Anglo-Saxon British way of life which must be protected from being contaminated by it.

The anglocentric nature of the 'new racists' position also appears in their demand for the 'repatriation' of black people to their inferior countries of origin. Repatriation is being used to camouflage the 'new racists' assessment of the black British way of life as inferior; to resist the possibility of the black British way of life influencing the white Anglo-Saxon British one; and to prevent black people and white people from establishing egalitarian relationships with one another. Through repatriation, the 'new racists' are proclaiming a subtle form of apartheid which will be concealed by sending black people 'back home'. Similarly, non-Anglo-Saxon white people are only acceptable as long as they assimilate into the white Anglo-Saxon British way of life. 'Aliens', i.e. non-Anglo-Saxon ethnic minorities from America and Europe, are no more wanted than those from India and Hong Kong. Through this particular political philosophy the 'new racists' have found a way of restructuring social relations so that they affirm white Anglo-Saxon supremacy and ideological hegemony in a new, but 'natural' and incontestable form. This has further mystified social relations between black and white people, facilitating anew the use of racism in reproducing a racially stratified population over which the dominant white group can rule (Cohen, 1985).

The social control of black people as *black* people occurs through their interaction with racist social relations, causing their experience of class to be mediated through and by race. The intertwining of class and race differentiates black people's experience of class oppression from white people's (Gilroy, 1987). Similarly, black women's experience of gender is mediated through and by race (Bryan, 1985; Lorde, 1984; Carby, 1982). Consequently, their experience of sexism differs from white women's.

Racism is a socially constructed and reproduced historically specific phenomenon whose form changes in response to transformations occurring within society's socio-economic base, altering between periods of expansion when economic demand for cheap labour results in policies promoting overseas immigration, i.e. the importation of labour with settlement rights, and the reverse during recessionary phases (Dominelli, 1978b; Gilroy, 1987). Racism in the Britain of the 1980s is being restructured to take account of a declining manufacturing sphere within the context of international monopoly capitalism.

Using immigration as the regulatory mechanism to attract or reject overseas labour (Castles and Kossack, 1972), the British state participates in this process as both formulator and enforcer of immigration policy, and as an employer in its own right. Layton-Henry (1983) gives an account of how immigration policy shifted from heralding an open-door policy in the 1950s to demanding strict control by the 1970s as British capital's need for labour declined. The current economic crisis in Britain requires a restructuring of its labour force and a realignment of the balance between the internally generated labour force and that imported from overseas. The existence of a large, internally generated labour force consisting of unemployed waged workers, women working in the home, and unemployed youth obviates the need for an imported one.

Sivanandan (1976) attributes the state's increasing willingness to endorse moves aimed at repatriating blacks as part of the process whereby the size of the workforce is substantially reduced. Dominelli (1978b) argues the need to reduce the size of the labour force and decrease the costs of reproducing it, pushes the state in the direction of converting immigrant workers to migrant workers or repatriated workers. The latter option is extremely attractive in a situation in which the government deems the welfare state a luxury wastefully consuming the surplus necessary for capital accumulation (Minford, 1984; Gilder, 1982).

The economic circumstances of late capitalism make the exploitation of black ethnic minority groups different from that of other non-Anglo-Saxon ethnic minority groups of earlier periods. Besides the declining demand for their labour caused in absolute terms by the penetration of new capital intensive technology into the economy, many avenues of upward mobility previously available to other non-Anglo-Saxon ethnic minority groups are now closed off, locking black people into a permanent reserve workforce unless there is a substantial transformation in social relations.

Whilst structural analyses of racism are gaining currency in British academic circles, the bulk of the theories embodied in the field of 'race relations' focuses on descriptions of black communities and their inherent pathologies. Publications by white academics, eg. Rex, Tomlinson, Troyna, and Cashmore, have been criticised by Gilroy and others (CCCS, 1982; Gilroy, 1987) for presenting black people rather than racist social relations as the problem. Lawrence (1981) attacks black authors such as Foner, Khan, and Pryce, for pathologising black cultures and reinforcing racist notions of black people as inadequate, unintelligent, 'rural and backward', arguing their writings condemn black people for being ill-equipped to cope with white Anglo-Saxon British society. Their works also endorse expectations that black people need to be contained and controlled to not disrupt the smooth operation of society as a whole (Lawrence, 1981).

What are the parameters of anti-racist social work?

'What role is there for white people in eradicating personal, cultural and institutional racism in social work?' 'What policies and practices constitute the anti-racist social work which white people can follow?' 'How do we overcome the obstacles to our progress without reinforcing and reproducing racist social work practice ourselves?' 'How can we eliminate the institutional racism which bolsters and endorses our work?' I address these complex issues by arguing that fighting racism is white people's starting point in acknowledging that they have a different relationship to racism from black people, leading to different roles in the mutual project of dismantling it. White people's parameters are set by their position as creators and beneficiaries of racist social relations whether they engage directly in racist behaviour or not (Lorde, 1984). For by keeping black people out of direct competition with us and denying them access to goods and services, we get these regardless of our merit or need. In destroying the racist edifice we have constructed, we will lose the powers and privileges which we have gained at the expense of black people.

Black people's relationship to racism is a specific one in which as the oppressed, they confront its razor-sharp edge, struggle against it to minimise its pernicious impact on their lives, and elaborate the theory and practice of a black perspective in eradicating it (Gilroy, 1987). Black people share a common oppression which can unite them and provide a basis for collective action and solidarity between them. White people's common position as oppressors divides those fighting racism from white compatriots actively resisting anti-racist initiatives. Despite acting with greater sensitivity and awareness, the difficulties white people encounter in tackling racism are legion. We will make mistakes because white supremacy is such an integral part of our personalities and societal structures that we are often blind to its existence and perpetuate relations of domination when we are trying to eschew them. But we will also know when we have erred, for either our intuitive responses will signal it, or other white people will tell us, or black people will respond to us in ways which reveal we have been racist towards them, yet again.

Racism endorses injustice and damages both black and white people economically, socially and emotionally. Socially, racism distorts human relations between individuals and groups and makes all those involved poorer because honesty and openness are absent in the social interaction between them. The internalisation of supremacist ideologies causes deep psychological harm to whte people who assume superiority by virtue of the colour of their skin, and to black people who continually encounter racist onslaughts through being defined inferior. Economically, racism legitimates the exploitation of black people and inappropriate material gain for white people, and it causes society as a whole to lose out through the misuse of resources rightfully belonging to black people. Culturally, we miss out on the richness accruing from egalitarian relationships endorsing the celebration of diversity between peoples. Redressing the situation requires white people to counter the damage racism causes their personae and their relationships with black people by developing their role in fighting racism.

After taking responsibility for owning the monstrosity of racism, white people must actively deconstruct it. This constitutes the anti-racist struggle whereby white people can empower themselves. For me, this is a political, moral and socially necessary imperative. We must stop exploiting black people and desist from providing them with inappropriate services in exchange. In recognising the contribution black people make to our society and returning what is rightfully theirs, we become stronger and more complete people ourselves. For in getting rid of the injustice perpetrated by racism we will begin reclaiming our own humanity and establishing egalitarian relationships between black and white people. Thus, we have much to gain by eradicating racism. Anti-racist social work forms the bridge white people can cross to reach the competence required for them to begin working in non-racist, egalitarian ways with black people.

Though the processes whereby egalitarian relationships between black and white are achieved are difficult to develop, white people advocating anti-racist social work have a major input in redefining current definitions of social work along anti-racist lines. The lack of familiarity in working within egalitarian relationships and the loss of power over others will initially disorient and overwhelm white social work educators and practitioners. Neither our professional training which presupposes hierarchical relationships between ourselves and others, nor our previous experience will have prepared us for it. An acute awareness of our loss of power and privileges in the short-term will obscure the long-term advantages accruing from the implementation of an anti-racist stance. Yet white social workers will have to create egalitarian relationships with black people if they wish to work according to anti-racist tenets and become involved with black people working in similar directions. The bases on which white people can engage with black people in these processes will be qualitatively different from those currently defining interaction between black people and white people, as power imbalances arising from relations of domination will have to be eliminated from the outset.

White social work practitioners and educators may find it useful to discuss their contributions to the anti-racist struggle in social work and share their anxieties about how to move forward with colleagues who have attempted to develop such working relationships. For example, white anti-racist social workers in Hackney, Lewisham and Brent, and white anti-racist social work educators at Birmingham Polytechnic have learnt lessons and gained support from others through discussion. If white social workers start relating to black people on the basis of equality, not only will they be transformed into better practitioners all round, but their agencies' policies and practice will be similarly affected. The same holds true for white social work educators.

White social workers' relationships with white clients are suspect from the anti-racist perspective because the racism of disadvantaged white clients becomes particularly difficult

for the white social workers sympathising with their predicament to handle appropriately. For example, Emecheta
(1983), speaking as a black woman, describes how easily her
white social worker ignores the racial dimension in the
interaction between them, and glosses over the issue when
hearing her white clients' racist remarks. Looking at the
problem in microcosm, Cohen (1985) reveals how difficult it
is for white anti-racist youth workers to deal with racist
white lads in a run-down working class community despite
their being explicitly charged with establishing anti-racist
youth work. Similarly in community work, the account of
tenants' associations striving to implement anti-racist
practices in Tower Hamlets portrays the countless obstacles
white people have to overcome in establishing anti-racist
relationships (THTA, 1987). In all these accounts, white
social/community workers' uncritical acceptance of the premise that poor whites require a sevice makes them accord
fighting racism a lower priority than meeting white client
needs when the two objectives conflict with each other.
The dilemmas white social workers encounter in these
situations arise from their acceptance of white clients as the
'deserving poor' and the collusion engendered by their
shared assumptions of white supremacy. Comments like
'You only get a . . . service in this office if you're black',
following the declaration of an equal opportunities policy,
illustrate the point.

Ultimately, an anti-racist analysis implies that besides
changing social work practice, the society within which
social work is situated needs changing. Moreover, change
must occur on two fronts – the personal and the structural –
simultaneously. Finally, the nature of such changes is so
fundamental that ameliorating the position of black people
by eradicating racism leads to a substantive improvement in
the welfare of all people, irrespective of 'race'.

Consequently, to become fully human and live in egalitarian harmony with black people, white people have to
become anti-racist. Anti-racism is a state of mind, feeling,
political commitment and action. There is important work
for white people to do. The days when we could assuage our
guilt by employing black people to take up the anti-racist

struggle in social work on our behalf are over. In some situations, black people are refusing to endorse the tokenism of many of our gestures aimed at making good our inadequacies and concentrating their energies on their own communities. In other instances, because of the very nature of racism, change from within cannot be initiated by black people because they have been excluded from those very institutions and decision-making processes which oppress them. It is up to us who are there to change such situations by developing alliances and strategies which will foster anti-racist policies and practices.

In this book I examine what white social work practitioners and educators can and must do in struggling against racism in social work and developing non-racist social work in a number of settings – social services, probation, community work and the voluntary sector. I take the view that racism aimed specifically at non-Anglo-Saxon people forms part of a larger process of social control. Thus, it reinforces the controlling dimension of social work and intensifies the policing aspect of white social workers' relationships with ethnic minority groups and contributes to their exclusion from the creation and delivery of services relevant to their welfare. And, whether acknowledged or not, racism becomes a powerful rationing device in the hands of under-resourced social work agencies and training departments.

It is important that white social work practitioners and educators create a theory of racism contextualising social work within the state apparatus, understand the dynamics of racism in both its covert and overt forms, recognise its legitimation through social processes and institutions outside social work structures, and relate these to their everyday practice in social work – in what they do and what they don't do. Unravelling the dynamics of racism in social work practice becomes the preoccupation of Chapter 1. In it, I analyse racism at both personal and structural levels and link these directly to the personal prejudice and institutional racism evident in social work training and practice. I demonstrate how our very definitions of the social work task are imbued with and reproduce racism. Yet these features are virtually ignored in social work training. Overcoming the limitations this imposes on teaching, learning and practice requires white social work practitioners and educators as both perpetrators and beneficiaries of racism actively to engage in anti-racist social work and bring about the demise of racism in their areas of competence.

Existing social work education has had a major role in perpetuating social work theories and forms of intevention permeated by racism. This state of affairs will end when social work training accepts its central role in establishing anti-racist social work as the form of social work practised by future generations of social workers. Similarly, it has a key part to play in retraining existing social workers. Chapter 2, therefore, examines the racist underpinnings of social work training and education and makes suggestions for re-orienting training in anti-racist directions.

Social workers use their personalities, sense of self, and experience in establishing relationships with users of their services (Compton and Galaway, 1975). Because working in this manner is such a significant feature of social work practice, white social workers should question their cosy assumpions about their way of life, place in the world and views about black people. Embarking on and engaging in this process constitutes the anti-racism awareness or consciousness-raising stage in the struggle for establishing anti-racist social work. White social workers need to parti-cipate in this process before proceeding to the next step, i.e. taking action to transform their racist beliefs and stereo-types, and agency policy and practice. Without promoting change eradicating racism, anti-racism awareness is useless. It merely paralyses white social workers, leaving society's racist edifice intact. Chapter 3 considers anti-racism aware-ness training and its potential as a consciousness-raising activity aimed at combining heightened personal awareness of racism with anti-racist action at both person and structural levels.

Having completed this analysis, I focus the anti-racist perspective on a key milieu for social work intervention – the family. Chapter 4 examines the racist underpinnings of white social workers' current practice within black families, identifying the dilemmas they must resolve whether they are working with children, or women, or youths or elders. Using case material, it provides guidelines for the limited intervention white workers can appropriately undertake. Although I focus on the family because it is the prime site for social work intervention, the dynamics of racism operating within this milieu are replicated elsewhere, making the general lessons learnt in this arena transferable to other work with black individuals, groups and communities.

White social workers' anxieties about their involvement in anti-racist social work become particularly frustrating when they struggle as isolated individuals, or when they construe change as being limited to their particular agency. Overcoming the isolation of individualist responses requires white social workers to develop collective strategies coupling solidariy with material and emotional support from others. Forming support groups, networks and alliances is a prerequisite for the implementation of anti-racist organisational strategies in social work. Chapter 5 explores the implications of collective action by considering white social workers' involvement in eliminating racism in their workplace. It highlights the importance of reaching beyond their own agency to secure changes there by making alliances with people pursuing similar goals in other settings. Moreover, they will have to connect what is happening in their agency with central and local government policy and actions. Chapter 6 continues the exploration of organisational change by examining the role of white social workers in campaigning for anti-racist social work and laying foundations for transforming current practice. In Chapter 7, I conclude by considering the development of anti-racist/non-racist social work. Non-racist social work is about creating new forms of social work which transcend racism so that black and white social work practitioners and educators can work collectively together as equal partners in relationships free from racism.

Hence, this book is offered in the hopes of getting white social work educators and practitioners talking to one another individually and collectively about why they should become engaged in anti-racist social work and how they might best contribute to its achievement. It is not the final word in that process, merely a beginning whereby white people can undertake their own anti-racist initiatives instead of parasitically relying on black people to carry their burden of realising good anti-racist social work as one element in eradicating racism from the face of the earth.

1

Racism Permeates Social Work Ideology and Practice

White social workers' fond belief in their liberalism and non-judgmental openmindness is endorsed in a study by Bagley and Young (1982). This suggests social workers are more 'racially tolerant' than the general populace because only 3 per cent of them are racialist, i.e. hold crude racist views, compared to 20 per cent of the population as a whole. By identifying racism primarily in its overt forms, this definition of racism endorses its manifestation as the preserve of fanatical right-wing movements, groups and individuals. Making racism in social work practice a matter of individual import ignores the role of institutionalised racism and discounts the significance of indirect or unintentional racism. It pathologises the overtly racist few, ignores the subtle racism of the majority, and obscures the interconnections between structural forces and personal behaviour. Moreover, it converts racism into a matter which can be educated away, thereby ignoring the link between its eradication and the transformation of our socio-economic and political structures. And because only a 'few' white social workers are considered racist, it condones the belief that anti-racist struggles are activities which white social workers undertake either as an educational exercise aimed at promoting understanding of other people and their cultures, or as political activities undertaken outside working hours.

This chapter explores the way in which racism, an integral feature of British society, permeates social work from its ideological underpinnings through to its practice, and demonstrates how conceptualising racism as the irrational

21

beliefs of an evil few is misguided. With racism as the subtle playing-out of relations of subordination and domination in respect of 'race' in everyday routines and the minutiae of life, no aspect of social work is free from it. This makes it extremely difficult for white social work practitioners and educators to stand back from it and not become entangled in processes reinforcing its existence and endorsing its continuation. Colluding with racist policies and practices is the norm.

Racism in British society and social work: a theoretical and practical understanding

Racial inequality is the physical manifestation of the prevalence of racism in social relations. The structural nature of black people's plight has been affirmed through public inquiries (Scarman, 1982; Gifford, 1986) and research (Rose, 1968; Smith, 1976; Brown, 1984). Inegalitarianism disproportionately affects black people's access to social resources such as housing, employment and education (HMSO, 1981). Black people live in overcrowded inner-city areas, work in low-paid jobs without acquiring employment commensurate with their qualifications and skills, and experience higher rates of unemployment than their white counterparts regardless of their age, gender or class. Racism's pernicious threads permeate the whole fibre of the welfare state (CRE, 1985; Gordon and Newnham, 1985) despite the welfare state's commitment to helping the disadvantaged and those in need. Black people's limited access to the personal social services throughout their life cycle has been well publicised. The report, *Multi-Racial Britain: The Social Services Response* (ADSS/CRE), and Cheetham's (1981) report for the DHSS are only two of the numerous documents indicating that, despite known needs, black people are under-represented as recipients of personal social services. Others have demonstrated discrimination in health service provisions (Littlewood and Lipsedge, 1982; Malek, 1986), social security (Gordon, 1986), immigration (Foot, 1965; Layton-Henry, 1985), and probation (Taylor, 1981).

Authors have also highlighted the over-representation of black people in schools for the educationally subnormal (Coard, 1971), criminal proceedings (Tipler, 1986; AFFOR, 1978), and the higher echelons of the tariff system of court sentences (Dominelli, 1983; Home Office, 1986).

Black people also have little access to influential positions in the decision-making structures of both central state and local government levels, trade union organisations, or prestigious jobs. After an absence of 58 years, 4 black candidates have been elected to parliament in 1987. Few councillors are black. For example, although Sandwell's population is 11.4 per cent black, only four black people have become local representatives. Moreover, the Council holds a poor record as an equal opportunity employer. Only between 1 per cent and 2 per cent of its employees are black, and few of these are found at senior levels (*Sunday Times*, 15 April 1984). Our large cities including London have an equally appalling record. Although some authorities have encouraged black people to enter their ranks at the highest levels, these have had limited impact. Only a few social services departments in Greater London have had black people reaching the top echelons of management. There are many areas of public life in which blacks are conspicuous by their absence. Even in the higher reaches of the trade union bureaucracy it is the same, despite the disproportionately high number of black workers found within the trade union movement (GLC, 1984).

The experience of black people is that of welfare disenfranchisees being bombarded with systematic discrimination, a denigration of their cultural achievements and humiliation if they dare rise above their alloted place (CCCS, 1982), despite reassurances from government leaders guaranteeing them equality of treatment, justice and dignity.

Racism takes white norms as the measuring rod of life and accords worth and dignity to blue-eyed, blonde-haired, light-skinned individuals, granting those having these characteristics beauty, confidence and power. Those lacking these are made to feel ugly, dejected and powerless (Emecheta, 1983; Morrison, 1986). The social construction of black people's lives around their imputed worthlessness prepares the ground for their being pathologised and victimised. Morrison (1986) traces the impact of this powerful motif on the lives of black children in *The Bluest Eye*. Here, 'it is the blackness that accounts for, that creates, the vacuum edged with distaste in white eyes' (Morrison, 1986, p.48) when black people and white people interact. Being rejected by white people because of her skin colour, one of the book's black protagonists becomes desperate to acquire blue eyes and with them, acceptance and fulfilment. She is 'A little black girl who wants to rise up out of the pit of her blackness and see the world with blue eyes' (Morrison, 1986, p.161). Some of her companions refuse to be defined by the white yardstick, but they also find every aspect of their lives circumscribed by it, and have to exert considerable energy carving out the smallest space for themselves by opposing it. Speaking in oppositional terms when she is contemplating poverty and the destruction of black family life around her, one of them says: 'I felt a need for someone to want the black baby to live – just to counteract the universal love of white baby dolls, Shirley Temples, and Maureen Peals' (Morrison, 1986, p.176).

These extracts reveal that racism damages the oppressed economically, socially, politically and psychologically, whilst at the same time illiciting resistance to its ravages (see also Fanon, 1967; Bryan, 1985). Meanwhile, racism operates to the economic and political advantage of the oppressors who are oblivious of the havoc they are wreaking; the vacuum in their eyes signified the 'total absence of human recognition – the glazed separateness' (Morrison, 1986, p.47). As a form of social control, racism keeps people in their place and rations social resources according to their position in the social hierarchy.

White social workers should bear in mind the psychological damage racism imposes on black people who internalise the dominant values of a white society denigrating blackness when they are confronted with black nursery-school children wanting to paint their skins white (Coard, 1972), or black children in care demanding white foster parents, and not interpret such behaviour as manifestations of white superiority. Rather, such responses are often survival responses –

one way black people have found of surviving the daily onslaught on their racial integrity (Bromley, 1972). If white social workers can see such conduct as manifestations of resistance to racism, their response should be to take immediate steps to protect these children from further racist damage and to eradicate the racist practices which endorse and perpetuate such behaviour. Besides demanding that white people adopt anti-racist forms of practice that transform the nature of social work, dealing with these situations requires the employment of black social workers to make a proper assessment on the needs of black children and the placing of black children amongst black families living in black communities (BACSG, 1984). Making black dolls available to white children in nurseries, employing black staff in significant numbers in welfare agencies and placing them in positions of authority, and developing services appropriate to the needs of black people become meaningful as steps in tackling racism, not ends in themselves. For the end of the anti-racist project can only be achieved through the elimination of racism and the establishment of egalitarian social relations throughout society.

Immigration policy has been the major public arena in which the politics of race impinging on social work practice have been officially played out. This process has shifted immigration policy from being a matter of concern to immigration officials at the point of entry to the central mechanism for internal control (Gordon, 1984). These developments have subjected black people ordinarily resident in Britain and those born here to continual surveillance by the forces of 'law and order' and scrutiny by officers providing welfare services (Gordon, 1986; Gordon and Newnham, 1985). Immigration status is systematically used to deny black people living and working in Britain and paying its taxes, 'recourse to public funds', including national insurance benefits to which they have contributed, e.g. disallowance of unemployment benefit for those on work permits, child benefits for children living overseas, supplementary benefits for women whose husbands have gone on prolonged trips abroad to fulfil family obligations (Gordon and Newnham, 1985; Chapeltown, 1983).

The welfare state competes for governmental resources with capital accumulation and defence expenditure (Dominelli, 1978a). It loses out as long as the government defines public expenditure cuts in terms of limiting welfare provisions. In this context, stripping black people of their rights as citizens, curtailing the rights of 'immigrants' to welfare sevices, and encouraging their repatriation so that Third World countries foot the bill for their welfare, is economically sound and forms an integral part of Thatcherism's monetarist direction.

Social work's structural position in bearing its share of cuts imposed on the welfare state affects the roles social workers undertake, distorting client–worker relationships by diverting resources from the welfare arena, and skews the power balance between them away from those demanding services towards those providing one. Allocating resources away from the social reproduction of labour shifts the emphasis of social work intervention away from its caring concerns and orients it more forcefully towards its controlling ones.

The high visibility of black people makes it easier for them to be targeted as objects whose eligibility to service must be authenticated above and beyond 'normal' standards. A white social worker put this to me as follows: 'I worry about whether or not I should be providing welfare rights advice to Asian families coming into the office without asking for their passports first.' The possibility that these Asian families may be black British wholly entitled to welfare services is submerged by white social workers' anxieties that they are dealing with 'immigrants'. It is a racist position which gives black people the loud and clear message that they have not really been accepted as having a rightful place here.

Racism, therefore, saves the government considerable sums of money, and makes the Anglo-Saxon majority cautious about demanding welfare rights for themselves by fostering the view that individuals are solely responsible for their own welfare. The mystification of the reprehensible connection between the exclusion of 'immigrants' from welfare provisions and the public expenditure cuts occurs because white social workers limit their intervention to those having publicly legitimated access to their services. The uncritical acceptance of popular definitions of those having access to welfare services leads white social workers to condone and confirm certain myths which are firmly imbedded in immigration ideology and practice, e.g. black people are in Britain on a temporary basis; black people are born overseas; black people provide their own welfare systems. It also facilitates their participation in the provision of inappropriate services for black people, e.g. interpreters and home helps who are not matched for language, religion and caste.

The endorsement of racism at the highest political levels, e.g. Thatcher's speech about British people being 'swamped' by an 'alien' culture (*Daily Mail*, 31 January 1978) and the 1981 Nationality Act (Gordon, 1985) have intensified the legitimacy of the view that black people do not *belong* in Britain. Making racism 'respectable' exacerbates black people's feelings of vulnerability and authorises *laissez faire* attitudes and practice endorsing inappropriate service provision and poor service delivery.

The British state has a contradictory position with regard to racism. It has made racism respectable by enshrining it in nationality legislation which is enforced through immigration controls (CRE, 1985). It has recognised race as one dimension through which people can be disadvantaged and has tried to respond positively to its elimination by persuading people to accept equal opportunities for all by encouraging government bodies to adopt the status of 'Equal Opportunity Employer' and promulgating legislation aimed at doing so, e.g. the Race Relations Acts. But this legislation is difficult to enforce and does not merit the label 'anti-racist'.

The state's role in this process is neither a conspiratorial one nor a subordinate one in which it acts as the 'tool of the bourgeoisie'. Rather, the state as a whole is caught in the contradictory position of responding to the needs of the accumulation of capital on the one hand and the reproduction of labour power on the other (Dominelli, 1978a). However, Corrigan's (1976) argument that the class struggle mediates the outcome between the conflicting demands placed on the state by capital and labour needs refinement. The state itself, as one of Britain's largest employers and providers of welfare services, has a vested interest in the outcome of this struggle. Its position is further complicated by the struggles state employees have initiated and orchestrated over welfare provisions, e.g. industrial action by health service workers, fieldworkers and residential workers in social services, and teachers. Moreover, the relative autonomy confirmed on the state as mediator in these struggles gives it a certain independence from its roles in guaranteeing capital the conditions for accumulating wealth and workers their livelihoods. The direction in which that independence is channelled depends on who has control of the state apparatuses. Consequently, the extent to which ethnic minority groups organise in pursuit of their interests and the influence which anti-racist white people can amass is crucial in affecting the outcome of the struggle for power and influencing decisions taken by the state. The intractability of the problems posed by racism and the complexity of the political, sociological, psychological and economic forces embedded in racist social relations make a mockery of primarily economistic analysis condemning racism as false class consciousness, e.g. Cox (1970).

Social workers have an important role in both facilitating and initiating the process of empowering themselves and consumers in relation to the state by contributing to anti-racist struggles being conducted within as well as outside of the social work arena. For its objective of promoting people's welfare to be achieved, social work has to transcend the contradiction of providing for people's welfare whilst rationing resources amongst those 'deserving' help. Racism allows white social workers to straddle this contradiction by relegating black people to the realms of the 'undeserving' poor, making them welfare disenfranchisees with restricted access to welfare provisions.

In not confronting its own racism, social work practice belies the liberality of its ideology. Social work's failure to challenge its own racism can be attributed to its structural determinants. These are: its allegedly apolitical professional stance; its emphasis on social control at the expense of caring; its role in rationing scarce welfare resources; and the way in which it problematises ethnicity.

Racism in social work practice

a. *Racism exacerbates and extends social control in social work*

At the present time social work, like other elements in the welfare state, is being dismantled and restructured to exclude more and more people from receiving its provisions. Racist immigration laws, unfair checks on black people's entitlement to benefit, and the endorsement of a transient status for black people living in Britain have seriously reduced the number of black people claiming their share of welfare resources, despite their entitlement to do so (Gordon, 1986). Illustrating this process, a study by Harambee in Lewisham revealed that despite being entitled to benefits, 50 per cent of black youth did not claim any (CIS, 1978). This attitude is exacerbated by the derogatory treatment of black youths at the hands of DHSS officers. As one young black man told me, 'I'm not going in there to be treated like shit. And they give you nothing.'

In a climate of public expenditure cuts and the rationing of social services resources, the state becomes a force intensifying social workers' responsibilities as agents of social control whose task is to reduce demands for scarce public resources. The high visibility of certain ethnic groups, particularly black ones, makes it easier for them to be made scapegoats for the economic recession and to be targeted as subjects whose eligibility to services must be authenticated above and beyond 'normal' standards. This happens when black people are required to produce their passports in order to send their children to school or receive medical care.

Moreover, Mrs Thatcher's public expenditure cuts have reduced both the number of welfare workers and the material resources at the disposal of those remaining in the field (Loney, 1985). Meanwhile, demands for resources are mounting because of the pressures of unemployment and changing demographic structures. Consequently, social workers are more likely to be sucked into rationing resources to cover the largest number of clients, thereby improving efficiency, than to press for open-ended commitments to cover whatever 'needs' arise (Howe, 1986), making the criteria determining provisions economics rather than 'need'. Social workers find they have to refuse aids and adaptations, telephones, and home helps, in implementing 'community care' for older people because money is not available. The Social Fund will further restrict social workers' response to that encompassed by the resources at hand. Economic constraints and shifting eligibility criteria induce social workers and their managers to accept 'technical' rationing mechanisms which seem uncontentious, thus bypassing the political questions entailed in resolving questions of 'need'.

The reduced availability of resources carries particular implications for black people whose specific needs are given short shrift because they have been constituted as the 'undeserving poor'. The additional resources they need to bring them to the same base line as poor whites are unlikely to be forthcoming during a period of cuts. Treating black people 'the same as everyone else' means the deficit in resourcing between black and white will not be eliminated; it will remain unacknowledged. Moreover, abounding stereotypes of black people will ensure that questions about their needs will not be raised. For example, their not coming forward with claims for help will continue to be interpreted as their not requiring the services available rather than leading to an investigation of the relationship between white agencies and black people; the nature and appropriateness of the services on offer; the methods of informing them of their entitlements; and the attitudes towards their demands for help. Without questioning these, white social workers can remain convinced black people do not request their services because their community welfare networks look after them.

Within the framework of dwindling resources, the professional ethic and ideology of social work trap social workers in a further dilemma. How can social workers pay tribute to client self-determination and empower clients to acquire greater control over their lives whilst they operate under a state of siege? How can the conflict between black working-class people's need for resources and that of white working-class people be reconciled within diminishing resources? For example, how do white social workers adjudicate between the needs of a white older person needing sheltered housing and those of a black child requiring a day nursery place? It's much easier for them to avoid this quandary if they believe that relationships in black communities are such that someone will step in to care for the child. The failure of social work as a profession to confront this dilemma is problematic for both black and white workers. Concern over this issue compels black authors such as Gilroy (1987) to affirm the importance of black people controlling their own resources and autonomous spaces, whilst questioning the use of black self-help groups to perpetuate white people's view that 'black people can look after their own', thereby letting white people and institutionalised racism 'off the hook'. Thus, white social workers working in anti-racist ways have to consider racism in service delivery within a context in which the welfare state is being dismantled and restuctured to exclude more and more people from receiving welfare provisions.

b. Social work as an apolitical activity

The dilemma posed in choosing between the needs of a black and a white person reveals that social work is not an apolitical activity which can ignore power relations and the unequal distribution of resources in society. When developing anti-racist practice, white social workers have to take seriously the differential access social groups have to these, and become aware of the implications of power relations in their work with black individuals, groups and communities. This requires white social workers to recognise social work practice as a political activity in which power operates on a number of different levels, including the powers vested in them by society to allocate and distribute resources falling under their jurisdiction, the legal powers they hold as social workers, and the power relationships entered into with clients.

In addition, white social workers need to be ethnically sensitive to the different meanings ascribed to social inter-actions by people who follow different cultural traditions from theirs, and become attuned to the implications of their own dominant or majority ethnic culture on their practice. Furthermore, they need to be aware of the diversity con-tained within their own ethnic culture and that of other ethnic groups. By engaging with these, white social workers will become knowledgeable about themselves as individuals, their value systems and the way in which they legitimate relations endorsing white supremacy. Moreover, white social workers have to grapple with the constraints being state employees imposes on their doling out scarce res-ources. For these establish boundaries around the choices open to them and their clients which are difficult to tran-scend (Simpkin, 1980). Additionally, their vulnerability as employees is increased if they adopt overtly political stances placing them at odds with either agency or state objectives. This latter consideration is crucial in situations in which the state itself furthers racist practices through specific social policy measures.

c.   *The obstacle of professionalism*

Professionalism in social work practice has been elaborated on the premises that social workers have 'faith in the system' (Compton and Galaway, 1975, p.34), maintain their dis-tance from clients, and do not get involved in 'political' issues. A professional social worker is not interested in challenging the social structures in which the social work task occurs and remains objectively neutral on the major social concerns of the day during work-time. Since racism is deemed one such issue, white social workers either ignore its existence or do not concern themselves directly with it. Hence, they work with black clients on the same basis as white clients, inadvertently reproducing racist policies and practice.

Social workers are expected to deal with people by empathising with their condition, according them respect and dignity, and facilitating their access to the resources and expertise they need to assume control over their lives (Compton and Galaway, 1975). But this position is difficult for them to achieve in normal relationships with clients. For example, Seebohm (1968) revealed that 60 per cent of social work clients had financial problems which social workers needed to address. Whilst social workers may be underpaid, they do not have the same financial starting point as their clients. This may undermine their capacity for empathy. Additionally, social workers lack the resources necessary for responding to cries for financial aid. As one angry woman on probation for shoplifting informed me: 'My probation officer's useless. I need money to feed my kids. Not tea and sympathy. But I know he's got none to give me. So he tells me to behave myself and not get into trouble again.'

Whilst social workers currently have access to Section 1 money and will shortly be involved in decisions concerning the allocation of Social Fund monies, these sources alone are incapable of meeting clients' financial requirements. Thus social workers often find themselves in the frustrating position of knowing what clients need, but feeling hopelessly unable to help them achieve it. Therefore they become involved in 'papering over the cracks' and making 'poverty seem the client's fault' (Bailey and Brake, 1975), thereby engendering the social control of their clients and their aspirations. As their attention is deflected onto resolving 'clients' personal problems', social workers expend considerable energy teaching clients to change their behaviour, making it conform more closely to 'acceptable' standards. For black clients, this has led white social workers to ignore the specific circumstances and avenues through which racism holds black people back and deprives them of resources, power, justice and dignity. As one young Afro-Caribbean man I interviewed said:

I got done with TWOC [stealing a motor car] a few years back and sent to borstal for 6 months. About a year later, this fancy Porsche was nicked not far from here. The police came banging on my door, saying I'd done it. I hadn't. I had me own car by then. I'd got this job you see. But they keep coming round anytime anything happens. And it's not 'cause they know me, it's 'cause I'm black. I was driving this brand new car once – a Rover I'd borrowed from a mate. And the police stopped me. Wouldn't believe my story. They said, 'People like you don't buy cars like this.' And they charged me . . . My probation officer said, 'I shouldn't worry about it. The police were just doing their job. They were wondering where people like you get money to buy expensive cars.' He then asked me if I sold drugs to get all the nice things me and my girlfriend had in the house. I got real mad. And he said he was joking!

The failure of white social workers to take on board the specific conditions affecting black people has meant that they have colluded with the continued denial of their access to resources, dignity and justice. In another example, an Afro-Caribbean woman left her two young children with their Afro-Caribbean father to work temporarily on the Continent. Shortly after her departure, the man also found a job. He tried desperately hard to get help with the childcare, but was not successful. So he found himself juggling several timetables trying to manage on his own. After a while, the children started truanting from school and were eventually caught stealing goods from the local market. A white social worker speaking with the father asked how he was going to ensure the kids attended school and did not get into trouble. 'Was he going to call his "wife" back?' He explained he could not and asked what facilities social services could offer. When he was told 'none', he insisted that he be given support. But the white social worker replied: 'Why don't you ask a member of your extended family to help you with them? You Africans are always looking after each other's children.'

Additionally, white social workers' concern to get clients behaving appropriately has problematised ethnicity by judging black people according to dominant stereotypes of their ethnic grouping. Belonging to an 'inferior' ethnic group means automatically being defined a problem by white social workers. The following illustrates the point. A young Afro-Caribbean man was charged with 'causing grievous bodily harm' during an affray. The probation officer who was asked to complete a social enquiry report on him said: 'Another one of those! West Indians are always getting into difficulties. They've such violent tempers. They flash at the drop of a hat. You've got to be ever so careful with them.'

Social work's poor showing on racism indicates the intractability of the problems confronting anti-racist social workers and trainers. And it means that to combat racism, white social workers and educators must adopt political and theoretical perspectives which are more than just ethnically sensitive. They must produce theories of welfare which acknowledge social work's social control function; recognise its dual position within state structures – a controller of substantial resources and the upholder of a caring ideology; and promote anti-racist social work practice. Thus, *to develop anti-racist social work, we need to cut the Gordian knot of social work as a complex and contradictory form of social control*.

Anti-racist social work is not a case of simply adding 'race' onto our considerations of a basically benign social work. What is required is the transformation of social work practice through the creation of social relations fostering racial equality and justice. To move in this direction, social work has publicly to adopt a political stance against racism on cultural, institutional and personal levels within practice, social work education, and the state apparatus more generally, thereby beginning the process of ending racism perpetrated and legitimated by the state itself, and challenging a professionalism whose neutrality disguises support for the status quo. Professionalism will have to be redefined in terms of white practitioners taking sides against practices endorsing racial oppression, and transforming their work.

Meanwhile, white social workers' failure to acknowledge the more subtle and covert forms of racism permeating practice has resulted in their unwittingly exacerbating black people's experience of racism. White social workers reinforce racism during service delivery through: a) the intentional and unintentional use of racism as a form of social control aimed at keeping black people in their place; b) the perpetuation of universalistic (the same service for everyone) treatment of all client groups, thereby ignoring the extreme hardship endured by black people; and c) overtly racist practices.

d.   The colour-blind approach and the universality of treatment

Social workers have incorporated racist elements in their practice by adopting the view that black people are like white people. Referred to as the *colour-blind approach*, its dynamics cover far more than those whereby white social workers ignore the colour of black people's skin. It is not that white social workers are unaware of the colour of a person's skin, but that they discount its significance. Or, as they have put it to me: 'Race is unimportant. Knowing them as people is'; 'I treat black people and white people the same. We are all members of the human race. There are no differences between people for me.'

Colour-blindness is expressed primarily through the concept of 'universality of treatment' whereby equality is assumed rather than proven because all individuals and groups are treated as if they were 'all the same'. This reduces everyone to the same common denominator, without regard to their actual material position either as individuals or as members of a specific social grouping. Little account is taken of the lower socio-economic position occupied by black people; their different cultural traditions, familial organisation and obligations, and attitudes towards life, society and its social institutions; the variety and heterogeneity in their midst; and the systematic and systemic racism they endure daily. On occasion, these differences may be recognised. But these are judged inferior to those of white people, so pressure is put on black people to conform either to white people's standards or to their stereotypes of them.

Besides ignoring the structural inequality defining the opportunities available to black people, this approach is rooted in white supremacy. Only those belonging to the dominant group enjoy the privilege of discounting the difference 'race' makes to the quality of service available to them and their access to it. The colour-blind approach is conceptually linked to the 'new racism'. Both harbour the idea that individuals and groups need not specifically refer to 'race' because it is visually obvious which 'race' is being considered, and the underlying assumptions about 'race' do not need spelling out. The colour-blind approach also contains a dynamic forming an integral part of relations endorsing white supremacy. That is, compelling all individuals and groups to conform to 'desirable' behaviour. Its standards are compatible with maintaining bourgeois hegemony, i.e. endorsing white middle-class heterosexuality. In social work intervention with black people, this is evident when white social workers try to make black individuals, families, or communities, like white ones.

White social workers' training, professional ethics, and their service delivery lend credence to the view that apart from relatively insignificant individual differences which can be subsumed through individual casework, the British population is largely homogeneous and racial factors unimportant (Cheetham, 1972). Hence, practitioners assume universalistic treatment is the best basis for preserving equality amongst individuals (ADSS/CRE, 1978). Even those social workers recently seeking to achieve 'ethnic sensitivity' and reflect multi-cultural dimensions in their work have continued to treat individuals from a particular ethnic group as 'all the same'. For example, whilst being aware that the experience of a Jamaican is different from a Nigerian, an 'ethnically sensitive' social worker tends to perceive the experience of all Jamaicans as similar. Besides 'race', 'universality of treatment' ignores the effects of other social divisions, e.g. gender and class, on individual circumstances. Women clients' attention is focused on their responsibility to care for children and men (Wilson, 1977). Working-class people are exhorted to emulate white middle-class life-styles without having access to similar resources (Bailey and Brake, 1975). The convergence between these social divisions and the universality principle grant white, upper-class Anglo-Saxon males the most advantage, and black working-class women the least.

The *universality of treatment* and uncritical casework approach to their task has resulted in white social workers contributing a further dimension to the racist burden already borne by black clients through discrimination in other parts of the welfare state and immigration controls. Thus, black people's welfare is jeopardised by the very institutions whose responsibility it is to promote them.

Besides preventing white social workers from seeing for themselves the significance of bringing black clients to the same socio-economic starting line as white clients, the universality principle inhibits their ability to explain the need for doing so to others. Yet recognising the gap between black working-class people's access to power and resources and that of the white working class is essential to stemming the backlash from poor working-class whites who feel they are also disadvantaged. Whilst both black and white working-class people experience deprivation because of class, only black people are denied power and resources because of their race. The connection between class and race accounts for the disparity between them. Recognition of such differences and the points from which they stem is essential in promoting racial equality. The formation of alliances between black organisations and white working-class ones more generally is problematic because racism permeates the white working class which also benefits from racism (CCCS, 1982). The rationing of resources legitimated by racism means white working-class people do not compete for scarce resources with black people who have been excluded as 'undeserving'. Hence, the distribution system does not encompass black people and the few privileges or resources available for distribution within the working class go to white people. Resources are allocated to individuals because they are members of a specific group with acknowledged access to these. Individual merit become secondary, if not irrelevant.

White social workers demanding resources for one individual case involving black people, are wide of the mark, even if they succeed in getting what they want, for every other black person faces discrimination from a similar source – racism. For example, a white social worker wanting housing for a black family will discover their being a *black* family is crucial to the housing authority's response. In housing allocation policies, the criteria regarding intentional homelessness are applied against that family as a *black* family. Various assumptions about black families' immigration status, size and links with their communities impinge on their rights to public housing. These are taken into account in ways which exclude them from the best council housing stock, from repayment mortgages, and desirable residential areas (CRE, 1985; Jacobs, 1985), as has happened to Bangladeshi families in Tower Hamlets. They were denied council housing for having made themselves intentionally homeless by emigrating to Britain (*Guardian*, 28 April 1987). Against this backdrop, white social workers appealing for 'positive discrimination' for black people confuse the issue. Black people do not require 'positive discrimination' because, as white people frequently allege, they lack qualifications and experience. Rather, they demand the elimination of racism because they are systematically discriminated against and have both their qualifications and experience denigrated. It is this systematic discrimination which must be eradicated.

Racism in social work: a social issue

White social workers wishing to eliminate racism in their practice, must make racism in social work a social issue and ally themselves individually and as a group with progressive, anti-racist forces within both the state apparatus generally and social work. They can take direct initiatives in organising these forces, and use their membership of political organisations, trade unions, professional associations, employing authorities and training bodies, to those ends, as some have done already through NAPO and NALGO. Only by continual vigilance and action against the racism perpetuated by themselves and those organisations and bodies which govern on their behalf, can white social workers begin to dent the racist bulwark underpinning social work.

White social workers adopting an anti-racist position have a consciousness-raising role in making white people perceive racism as a social issue. Their day-to-day interactions with black people living in decaying urban areas resisting their poverty and coming to grips with hardship puts them in a position of being able to counter racist claims that black people are responsible for creating their own problems. They can challenge such allegations by using their practice experience to demonstrate the resilience of black people in overcoming adversity. It also enables such social workers to participate in public debates about poverty, its social causes, its debilitating effects on individual personalities, and its destructive impact on black–white relationships. And, they can use these experiences to argue for the transformation of social work practice in accordance with egalitarian anti-racist principles.

In this I am conveying a different message from the one white people normally communicate to black people. I am saying the responsibility of dismantling society's racist edifice belongs to white people who enjoy the privileges emanating from it. The primary task of white social workers wishing to implement anti-racist practice is to change their own racist attitudes and practices and those of the organisations within which they work. Black social workers could spend their time organising to get resources for black communities instead of exhausting their energies on helping white social workers overcome their own racism.

Meanwhile, black people have not been passive in the face of racist onslaughts against them. They have organised themselves as black people to defend their interests, challenge white people's understanding of their oppression, and demand an end to personal, institutional and cultural racism (Moore, 1978; CCCS, 1982; Gilroy, 1987). White people need to respond positively to the anti-racist agenda black people have placed before us.

2

Social Work Training is Imbued with Racism

Social work education has done little in challenging the racism inherent in its theories and practice. Although it has published several documents on the matter, the Central Council for Education and Training in Social Work (CCETSW) has failed to ensure that anti-racist measures become a compulsory part of the curriculum. Thus subject disciplines are based on anglocentric models which take white British culture, history and achievements as the norm. Psychological theory and human development is considered largely in terms of the white British male standard. Discussions about the family centre on the white middle-class heterosexual nuclear family as the favoured type. Variations from this are deemed 'deviant' and consequently undesirable (Eichler, 1983; Segal, 1983; Lorde, 1984). Social policy is invariably British, glorifying white British processes and institutions. Unacknowledged racism has been a central theme in the theories and ideologies used in setting up the British welfare state and characterises all post-war social policy (Williams, 1987). Law teaching ignores the racist dimension in the implementation of legislation (Gordon, 1984), and the racist bases on which it is formulated (Layton-Henry, 1985). Thus the epistemological base and political philosophy of social work education endorses the status quo, of which racism is an integral feature. Also, practice placements are not geared to training students in anti-racist social work since work countering racism is not specifically included in the student's proramme. Anti-racist policies are usually lacking in placement agencies. White practice

41

teachers are poorly equipped to provide adequate supervision for anti-racist social work; black practice teachers are conspicuously lacking. CCETSW has failed to make an anti-racist stance permeate its own structures by employing sufficient numbers of black staff either in its policy-making structures (by 1986, only one Council member was black), or in its staff composition. Neither has it demanded teaching staff on CCETSW validated courses reflect the makeup of society.

The social work curriculum: an analysis of the racism permeating the social work literature

The social work literature, though espousing a liberal democratic commitment to equality for all, has been remiss in its handling of racism as an issue. The failure of social work theories to specifically address racism has been reflected in the forms of practice they espouse. Jansari (1980) and Denney (1983), reviewing the social work literature, have indicated how limited the treatment of racism has been. But the issue transcends this, for *even literature aiming quite hard not to do so, unintentionally reproduces racist stereotypes and biases*. For example, despite the authors' intentions in a recent publication, *Race and Social Work* (Coombe and Little, 1987), section II suggests black people's culture is responsible for the racist treatment they receive. Black people continue to be the problem, as the following quote exemplifies:

> Because of the nature of their employment and the cultural restrictions imposed on them, the majority of first-generation Cypriots – more women than men – have had little opportunity to mix with the mainstream society and learn the English language. As mentioned above, children with non-English-speaking parents begin school at a disadvantage, which may impair their educational performance. (Orphanides in Coombe and Little, 1987, p.84).

As the problem is located amongst the Cypriot parents via their failure to learn English, the question of why English society failed to welcome Cypriot people into its midst and provide them with non-stigamtised resources for both learning English and retaining the Cypriot sense of cultural identity is never formulated. The identification of the problem in the terms evoked by *Race and Social Work* enable racism committed by ommission to remain undetected.

Despite their intention of espousing 'good practice' with black people, an examination of the theory and practice expounded in exemplary classic texts on social work with black people reveals the impact of racism on black clients is largely ignored. *Social Work with Immigrants* (Cheetham, 1972) and *Social Work with Coloured Immigrants and Their Families* (Triseliotis, 1972) endorse the views that the number of black people in Britain should be limited and that helping them ought to be directed towards assimilating them into British society. The doctrine of assimilation assumes the superiority of the culture to which people are being assimilated, i.e. white British culture. Thus, these texts have encouraged white social workers to think of black people as *the problem* to be addressed, thereby unintentionally harming black people's interests.

Cheetham and Triseliotis defined black people as 'reluctant settlers' who are imposing a 'burden' on social services, a claim feeding off the public's hysteria on 'race' at the time, but unsupported by the facts. Black people have made a positive choice in coming to Britain, seizing it as an opportunity to *improve their lot* in life (Ahmed, 1984). The majority of black people are economically active, thereby making few demands on social services (Ely and Denney, 1987). Besides, these texts ignore institutionalised racism in state policy and practice on immigration. The 1971 Immigration Act, passed whilst these books were being written, systematically undermined the rights of black people to enter Britain as *settlers*. Earlier legislation had denied Kenyan and Ugandan Asians holding British passports settlement rights. The 1962 Commonwealth Immigration Act had imposed restrictions on the previously unfettered right of Commonwealth Citizens to enter, settle and work in Britain (Layton-Henry, 1985).

These classic texts also reinforce racism through their conceptualisation of the social work task. Social work as casework is imbued with counselling techniques, focusing on individual clients and assuming that 'immigrant' clients are the same as other clients except for having *more* of the problems with which caseworkers are already acquainted (Cheetham, 1972). These similarities, (white) social work educators contend, make (white) practitioners' existing experience adequate preparation for working with black people.

But the experiences of black people at the time and subsequently have denied the validity of this approach to social work intervention (see Emecheta, 1983; Riley, 1985). From their black perspective, Cheetham's understanding of the social work task is misconceived. Firstly, it ignores the fact that it is primarily *white* social workers constructing a casework relationship with *black* people, thereby decontextualising 'race' and obscuring the power differential and privileges accessible to white professionals but not black clients. This criticism might have been less serious if white social workers had used it to create a breathing space for becoming aware of the significance of the racist dynamics operating in the casework relationship. Unfortunately, despite black people's endeavours in highlighting this point (see Gitterman and Schaeffer, 1972; Mizio, 1972; Kadushin, 1972), this definition of the social work task remains dominant in both educational establishment and the field.

In treating black people in the same way as white people, white social workers ignore the impact of the power imbalance above and beyond that emanating from their position as professionals in the relationship between them. Moreover, its persistence reveals that those who are in power need neither justify their use of power, nor do they spontaneously challenge it themselves. Secondly, these strictures mystify the position of black people. Black people do *not* have the *same* problems as white people. *White people's right to be in Britain is not being questioned. They belong here. Black people do not. They are guests.* The host–guest relationship underpinning black–white interaction reinforces the power of the former over the latter who are in Britain on their host's sufferance. Moreover, though unrecognised in classic texts, such an unequal relationship between black and white reinforces ideas about white supremacy.

Having not experienced rejection as an integral part of British society, white social workers are hard pushed to understand, let alone empathise with, the circumstances around which black people's lives are constructed. Moreover, since white social workers benefit from the existence of racism, they lack the material base from which to extend empathy to black people.

Such fundamental misunderstanding of black people's experience and the failure of white social workers to appreciate the power and privileges they enjoy because they live in a racist society facilitates their fostering racist stereotypes in their practice. Abundantly interspersed throughout the social work literature, these include stereotypes of: Asian women as passive and sexually repressed (Khan, 1979); Asian girls as 'caught between two cultures' (Triseliotis, 1972); West Indians as sexually promiscuous (Moynihan, 1965); West Indian parents as over-ambitious for their children and over-disciplinarian in their child rearing (Triseliotis, 1972); and West Indian families as unable to provide the environment in which the nuclear family prospers (Fitzherbert, 1967).

Social work texts are imbued with unexplored notions of white supremacy which are then translated into practice. The stereotypes they propagate provide useful motifs pathologising black individuals, families, communities and cultures, and portray black people as passive victims, taking whatever is hurled at them. For example, a Chinese student is considered 'blind to all expressions of anger and resentment' by her white placement supervisor because of the 'Chinese insistence on politeness and reverence' (Kent in Triseliotis, 1972, p.45). Emigration is deemed problematic. Firstly, it is termed 'migration', which suggests a temporal state of existence, i.e. black people are not here to stay. Secondly, 'migration' is blamed for the problems necessitating social work intervention. For example, the problems being experienced by Anthea, a West Indian child who skips school, and her family are assessed as 'the inevitable result of migration' (Cheetham in Triseliotis, 1972, p.63). The question of whether the school system is providing Anthea with their type of schooling she needs is never raised. The problem is located within the child and her family. By presenting black people in this light, these authors endorse the implicit assumption that (white) British institutions and culture are superior. Thus (white) social workers' task is defined as helping 'immigrants' come to terms with limited abilities and employment opportunities (Cheetham, 1972a, p.53); ignoring the damage racism inflicts psychologically and materially on black people. Meantime, black people are compelled to endure these tribulations as the price they pay for demonstrating their capability in 'coping' with life in difficult circumstances (see Emecheta, 1983). Racist policies and practices are camouflaged as the searchlight focuses on the qualities of black people themselves. Moreover, whilst highlighting the racial origins of clients, these texts do not identify those of their social workers. I have added the word (white) in the appropriate places because it is clear that the 'race' being ignored is white. The fact that these authors do not consider it important to specify the race of the workers explicitly in their statement is racist. The powerful are conscious neither of their position as such, nor of the privileges it bestows on them. Yet the failure to acknowledge racist dynamics in black–white interactions seriously hampers the possibility of establishing a real helping relationship between white workers and black clients (Gitterman and Schaeffer, 1972, p.286).

Moreover, it is not simply white social workers relying on casework techniques who perpetuate racist practice. White social workers doing groupwork and community work handle racism equally badly. The community work literature, e.g. *Current Issues in Community Work* (Gulbenkian, 1976), focuses primarily on (white) community workers working in small groups and neighbourhoods which are treated as homogeneous (white) units. Black authors have complained that white community workers fail to appreciate 'Their neighbourhood is invariably one which excludes "the blacks" who live next door or over the road' (Ohri and Manning, 1982, p.6). White community workers trying to counter racism in their activities do not root their efforts in either social structures or the specific relationships they establish with black people. Rather, they marginalise racism, treating it as the product of racial prejudices held by a small number of individuals. Racism thereby becomes an issue to be educated away through Multi-Racial Festivals (Ohri and Manning, 1982). The question white practitioners and social work educators have to address is not simply that the skills and methods expounded by orthodox social work theories are inadequate – the concepts embedded in these theories themselves are fallacious. What makes this realisation more worrying is that the anti-racist critique of social work cannot be confined to orthodox theories alone. The whole range of progressive social work analyses has been found wanting when measured by the anti-racist yardstick. The integrated methods approach typified by Pincus and Minahan in *Social Work Practice: Model and Method* has been criticized by Dominelli and McLeod (1982) for failing to specifically address racism. Amos, Carby and Parmar (1982) have highlighted the racist nature of white feminist theories. Feminist inattention to the issue in social work is exemplified in Brook and Davis, *Women, The Family and Social Work*. Social work texts written from a Left and/or Marxist perspective have paid scant attention to racism, e.g. Curno's *Political Issues in Community Work*; Simpkin's *Trapped Within Welfare*; Corrigan and Leonard's *Social Work Under Capitalism*; Bolger *et al*.'s *Towards a Socialist Welfare Practice*.

Examining the racism inherent in current definitions of social work

a.   The problematic of the casework approach

Defining the social work task in casework terms is a barrier to white social workers confronting racist practice because the social context of social work is ignored. Looking at the interpersonal dynamics within client–worker relationships is important because workers reproduce racist practices through their behaviour and collude with racist policies through their silence on the matter, but this is insufficient. The white social worker–black client relationship does not exist in a social vacuum untained by social, political and economic forces, although white practitioners operate as if it were, virtually without challenge in the literature white social work educators provide for them. Policies, treated as being outside the scope of the casework relationship, are taken as given. Individual practice is evaluated only from within its own framework of the services available and those actually provided without consideration of the services that ought to have been there. The casework approach pathologises white social workers who are blamed if their service is judged inappropriate by either supervisors or clients. This makes individual workers feel vulnerable, defensive and powerless in initiating change. It also obscures white social workers' responsibility in challenging power relationships, and puts the focus for change on the wrong target – white social workers' lack of knowledge of other cultures. Whilst overcoming white social workers' ignorance of non-Anglo-Saxon cultures is important in remedying their cultural insularity, defining overcoming racism as the removal of cultural gaps is an inadequate solution to the immensity of the problem being tackled and its complexities. Besides, cultural knowledge becomes a further avenue through which black people become pathologised (Ahmed, 1978; Gilroy, 1987; CCCS, 1982). For example, instead of seeing black people's decision to leave their dependents in their country of origin as a rational response to the lack of housing and uncertain job prospects facing them when arriving in Britain, white social workers define it as a negative cultural trait with a propensity to cause problems when the family is reunited (e.g. Cheetham in Triseliotis, 1972).

Moreover, casework professionalism portrays social work as a liberal profession graced with mutual tolerance and encourages white social workers to treat prejudice and discrimination as a matter of interpersonal dynamics, which can be quickly remedied by being educated away in classes describing the life-styles of different ethnic groups. But prejudice and discrimination feed off social conditions and their sanctification and legitimation in legal, political, social and cultural institutions. This makes for an interdependence and interconnection between the structural and the personal elements of racism, both of which must be tackled if racial oppression is to be eradicated.

Questioning the propensity of traditional casework to provide relevant services for black people, Cheetham subsequently moves away from casework-oriented 'social work with immigrants' to 'ethnically sensitive social work' which includes other social work methods such as community work and advice-giving (Cheetham, 1981, 1982). Although talking about (white) social workers' obligation to respond to the 'needs' of ethnic minority groups and to bring about organisational changes which will facilitate their doing so, Cheetham continues to ignore the significance of the workers' 'race'. This shift, whilst an advance on her previous position, remains problematic. Although highlighting the marginal positions black people occupy, she continues to pathologise them by holding them responsible for it (Cheetham, 1981, p.17), thereby blaming the victims of racism for their predicament.

Though carrying an expectation that organisational change will trigger off further changes, Cheetham's prescription oversimplifies the problem. It fails to include those changes in national policies and attitudes necessary for securing anti-racist organisational change in social work, e.g. immigration policies restricting black people's citizenship rights. It also neglects the importance of incorporating personal change in the organisational change process. Without this, commitment to ongoing reform will be lost amidst personal opposition emanating from racist white people. Personal change is essential for individual social workers fostering anti-racist social policy and practice. Furthermore, Cheetham naively assumes the welfare state is there to *meet people's needs*, thereby ignoring forces undermining that objective. In recent years this has included: the welfare state's control functions; the limitations imposed by public expenditure cuts; the withdrawal of 'discretionary' payments; the intensification of cuts following the Fowler Review and the 1986 Social Security Act; and the anticipated application of a 'residence test' which will deny black people access to social security benefits (LSSC, 1986). With dwindling welfare resources on hand, (white) social workers will find Cheetham's suggestion of becoming welfare rights advocates a puny mechanism for dealing with racism in social work.

An analysis aimed at eradicating such racism must examine the effects of cuts in welfare expenditure on the poorer sections of society. These must be balanced against increased public outlays on: 'law and order'; defence spending; subsidies to the private sector; tax relief for the better-off segments of society; and the hidden 'welfare' system of massive tax exemptions directing national taxation resources towards the wealthy, thereby revealing the class, race and gender biases in the social control apparatus, and demonstrating the inaccuracy of allegations that black people secure more than their fair share of resources through discrimination in their favour. Better-off white people continue to amass a disproportionate share of society's resources. White social work theorists going beyond 'race' and ethnicity to stress the total social construction of racism, can expose the falsity of such claims.

By considering the impact of racism on black people's lives more directly, Cheetham's lengthy introduction to the recent publication, *Social Work with Black Children and Their Families*, edited in collaboration with Ahmed and Small, is a substantial improvement on her earlier material. However, the book as a whole fails to transcend the limitations of traditional casework approaches to social work and lacks a theory of racism which contextualises social work within the broader society. Thus questions such as 'Why does social work perpetuate racism when it is supposedly geared to meeting people's welfare needs?', 'Why should social workers assume a political role by struggling against racism?', and 'What role can white social work practitioners and educators have in anti-racist social work?', are not asked. And the contradictions between responding to individual distress and overcoming structural constraints ignored in casework relationships remain unresolved.

b. *Cultural racism and the pathologising of individuals*
and cultures

The casework approach is riddled with cultural racism, i.e. the belief in the superiority of the Anglo-Saxon culture. This is apparent in attitudes which belittle black people's behavioural norms, and their expectations for improving their lot (Gilroy, 1987). Cultural racism is also reflected in white social workers' scepticism about black families' child-rearing practices; contempt for the close relationships between black parents and their children; and disdain in judging women's position within black families (Gilroy, 1987). Practices white social workers find tolerable amongst white clients become alarming among black clients, e.g. inter-generational conflict between parents and adolescents. Such behaviour, considered normal between white parents and their children, is defined as 'cultural conflict' in black families. Defining the problem thus legitimates intervention to 'free black children from the oppressive ties of their culture'. Healthy signs of black adolescents demonstrating independence and a questioning of parental authority are pathologised by white social workers (Ahmed, 1984), who subsequently subject black people to stricter surveillance and control, rapidly clientising them as a host of welfare agencies intervenes in their lives. Gilroy (1982) refers to this as 'differential intensity'. White social work educators struggling against racism should cease endorsing such practices in their teaching.

Some writers identify racism in social work practice as a white problem, e.g. Husband (1980a). However, his analysis lacks a historical perspective, fails to elaborate how class and gender interact with race, and provides social psychological explanations which include white social workers in the circle of pathology. They are blamed for not understanding the 'cultural traditions' of black people; not being sympathetic to their way of life; and not speaking their language. The onus is put on white social workers to change their behaviour and learn more about black people as *black* people. Whilst such measures are important in combating individual racism, it allows institutional racism to continue. Husband concludes that 'multi-racial social work is culturally competent casework, combined with organisational sensitivity to the needs of blacks'. Organisational change becomes a matter of 'sensitivity' grafted onto casework techniques. In failing to address the problem of racism as a construct of social organisation, culturally competent casework enmeshes black cultures in the tangle of pathology, and barely advances the struggle for developing anti-racist social work pratice. Husband's approach, like that of earlier writers, does not lead to the transformation of social work. Nor does it enable white social workers to question prevailing definitions of the social work task, and the structured inequality within which intervention occurs.

Social workers' willingness to practice culturally competent casework by learning about black people's cultures has been negatively redefined by the 'new racists' pulling together the pathologising of black cultures and the pathologising of white social workers. By criticising white social workers' failure to deal appropriately with the social problems confronting society and castigating social work's remote and bureaucratised professionalism, the 'new racists' have undermined social work's helping objectives, and redirected service delivery towards control and containment (Gilroy, 1987). The white media's handling of 'race' and crime statistics contributes to the pathologising process by conflating 'race' and 'crime' to endorse the view that blacks are responsible for Britain's 'high crime rate' as well as its economic decline (Hall, 1977). Consequently, the 'new racists' blame social work 'do-gooders' for helping clients, especially black clients, rather than being concerned with either society's objectives of 'maintaining law and order' or aiding the victims of client aggression, and use social work's general lack of support amongst the populace to link failed 'do-gooding' with permissiveness on race, scroungers, and law and order. Concerned with countering this perception of their work, the local state has pushed its local welfare agents, social workers, into more efficiently expediting their social control functions and containing the demands of more 'difficult' client groups. The emphasis on regulation and control has engaged social workers in 'policing' the black population, especially its problematic youth. Meanwhile, traditional social work values such as respect for individual civil rights are given short shrift. Social work educators should examine such issues as a central part of their teaching.

c.   *Multi-culturalism: a euphemism disguising racism*

The concept, 'multi-racial society', purports to convey the idea of equality in a pluralistic consensus. But conceptualising society in these terms assumes different racial and cultural groups are already equal, thereby defining racism away rather than dealing with it, and obscuring the necessity of having both black and white social workers confront racism as a structural and endemic feature of British society. Multi-cultural texts ignore structural inequality, and present black and white people as if they were already equal, with the main problem between them being not 'understanding cultural differences', e.g. Khan's *Minority Families in Britain*, Foner's *Jamaica Farewell*, Cashmore's *Rastaman*. These texts suggest that in the process of 'understanding these differences', black people and their cultures move towards white people and their culture. And they neglect the contradictions contained within social divisions, e.g. class, race and gender. Their underlying message endorses white supremacy, but each text handles it slightly differently.

Assuming that all members of society share the same political and economic troubles, Khan maintains that equal opportunities for black people are obstructed by individual attitudes, preferences and prejudices. Although she blames both sides for failing to advance the position of black people in Britain, she castigates Asian women for being 'backward', i.e. not sharing white values and traditions, and condemns them for being tied firmly to their roles as wives and mothers, even though this discounts their participation in waged work. Foner argues that Jamaican women prefer European physical features and habits and emulate these. This interpretation of Jamaican life devalues the day-to-day resistance offered by the majority of Jamaican women who do not follow white Anglo-Saxon fashions. Cashmore attributes the 'breakdown of law and order' amongst black youth to the disintegration of the West Indian family, thus adding to the chorus of voices pathologising this particular social unit. Moreover, he denigrates Rastafarian attempts to establish autonomous black organisations for withdrawing from society and hindering integration. Thus individuals trying to resist the racist chaos of the world around them by establishing alternatives to it are held responsible for their predicament.

The development of an anti-racist social work practice means taking on board the structured inequality existing between the different racial groups, and working on ways in which equality between them can be achieved. It requires white social workers to consider a multi-racial society as something that must be achieved rather than an entity which already exists. Treating British society as currently multi-racial means staying at the level of biology. Britain is multi-racial only in so far as it contains people with a variety of skin colours. It is not socially and politically multi-racial. Making British social work multi-racial requires white practitioners to move away from treating black clients as pathological individuals and acquiescent victims of social work. It also requires white social workers to acknowledge the politicisation of blacks. Black people know who they are and what is happening to them. And they are refusing to accept a form of social work intervention which exacerbates the intrusion of the state into their lives enabling it to exert greater control over how they lead them.

d.   *Pathologising black resistance to racism*

Other white authors have developed their understanding of social work's relationship with black people by looking more extensively at the black response to racism, at both individual and community levels. Whilst only a few, e.g. Wood (1974), focus on reintegrating blacks into the majority community, both white and black writers sharing a white perspective seize on cultural explanations to demonstrate black people's resistance is the problem. For example, in *Black Youth in Crisis*, Cashmore and Troyna consider the inappropriateness of black youth rioting in response to unemployment. Even the title suggests the crisis is occurring amongst black youth rather than within society and its organisation of social relations. This line of thinking is also evident in Pryce's *Endless Pressure*, where he talks about 'the problem of the second generation, alienated black youth'. Such explanations convert the social problem of racism to the problem of the response to it, thereby giving a new twist to pathologising black people – *pathologising black resistance to racism, whatever its form*. In belittling the black critique and response to their treatment, such inter-pretations of black activism perpetuate white social workers' failure to take seriously black people's critique of their work. This enables them to continue ignoring the ways in which racism is endorsed through their daily practice.

So, when hundreds of black youths, arrested following the 1981 rebellions, had their rights of *habeas corpus* and civil liberties ignored by the courts convened specifically to deal with them, white social workers and probation officers offered few objections. As one white social worker in Leeds told me, 'Rioting is not the sort of thing done in British society.' Yet if white youths had been treated en masse in this way, public outrage would have been ignited. The process is similarly replicated when white social workers deal with the individualised forms of black protest offered by Rastafaris. The Rastafari's stance against white racism is ignored by focusing attention of the individual's use of *ganja* and its illegality.

Within the probation service, matters are substantially worse. Social enquiry reports are littered with racist comments and stereotypes which do little to secure justice for black individuals (Whitehouse, 1985). White probation officers often feel unable to recommend sentences to the court because they 'do not understand black people and their ways'. They are afraid they 'cannot work with them on probation orders'. The final outcome of these positions is that black clients experience harsher sentencing (Pinder,

1984). Thus, black people are disproportionately represented in custodial settings (Home Office, 1986). Young blacks are less likely to receive cautions and be kept out of the processes leading to penal sentencing (Tipler, 1986). Even in the non-custodial area, Dominelli (1983) finds black people are more likely to receive community service orders for first and second offences, and be breached sooner for being absent from placements.

Autonomous black organisations must be respected by white anti-racist social work educators and practitioners

Anti-racist social work recognises the importance of black autonomy in enabling black people to develop their own structures and organisations against racism. Understanding this issue is crucial in the teaching of social work. Autonomous black organisations will supply the black practice teachers and lecturers necessary in training. Also, their staff will be articulating stringent critiques of current social work theories and practice. Autonomous organisation is essential if oppressed black groups are to exert their power to redefine their situation in society and take control of the process whereby solutions for their welfare are proposed. But, although black people have consistently lodged the legitimacy and appropriateness of their desire to organise autonomously to safeguard their interests in a racist society, white people respond to these suggestions with fear and label them 'separatist' (Phillips, 1982). The conflation of autonomous organisations with separatism in white people's minds arises from their attempts to resist moves which exclude them from controlling, i.e. subverting by incorporating into white supremacist structures, part of their reality. A white social work assistant on a training course clarified this issue for me when we were divided into a black group and a white group by saying: 'I don't understand why we [black and white people] can't join the same group. With them in their black group and us in our white group, it's like having apartheid in the classroom. It's another form of racism. We have the same aims in common. Why do they [course tutors] want to separate us?' Further discussion with this person revealed the anxiety that, 'I won't know what's going on in that [black] group and I can't influence it.' The point that black people have little power in shaping the outcome in white groups never struck that individual. Similar observations occurred during Gitterman and Schaeffer's analysis (1972, p.282) of working relationships between white workers and black clients: 'the white professional has the upper hand – both in the larger society and in the specific encounter between them.' As power dynamics are a crucial aspect of black–white interaction, white social workers must respect developments fostering black autonomy.

Autonomous black organisations, as oppositional forms facilitating black resistance to incorporation, have had a significant role in challenging existing service provisions and social relations in social work. White social work educators should be aware of such developments and reflect these in their teaching. Black professionals working from an autonomous base but integrated into mainstream services can both monitor current provisions for blacks and operate as a pressure group initiating change within mainstream social work. Models for activities attempting to redress the traditional power imbalance between black and white social workers are provided by the Black Families Unit in Lambeth and the Black Social Workers' Group in Hackney.

These models resemble apprenticeship learning. They require white social workers to subject their work to scrutiny and evaluation by black social workers operating as a group. The black social workers' monitoring group monitors and assesses the work of white practitioners for its racist content. White social workers have the task of working out how to change their practice, seeking help in developing anti-racist work from both black and white colleagues. The contribution of black social workers towards such training should be recognised as an integral part of their workload. Trade unions have the responsibility of ensuring this work forms part of black social workers' employment contracts. This requires NALGO and the other unions negotiating contracts for local authority workers to include countering racism in their collective bargaining process, thus redefining the tasks appropriately undertaken in workplace negotiations. Such initiatives also reveal how fighting racism carries implications for areas other than those being directly addressed.

Countering racism by having autonomous black organisations flourish within the existing welfare state is not the same as agreeing to the creation of separatist facilities for blacks. Arrangements based on separate provisions for black people carry the danger of condemning black people to an under-resourced and under-financed second-class service. Moreover, separatist provisions would involve black people in paying twice for services which are theirs by right – once through the general taxation system and once in direct payments to black organisations.

As the Lambeth and Hackney experiences demonstrate, autonomous black groups operating from within the framework of mainstream social services offer black professionals a collective identity and support networks through which they can enhance their power, facilitate their critiques of white colleagues' work; and effectively monitor and evaluate it. Such organisation reverses the customary flow of power between black and white professionals, and allows black people to demonstrate in practice their ability both to hold positions of authority over white people and to work co-operatively on a more egalitarian footing (Dominelli, 1979). Moreover, by organising their work in this fashion, black social workers avoid becoming trapped in the negative individualism and professionalism characterising much of white social workers' casework approach to social work (Stubbs, 1985). It also ensures that fighting racism is taken up as a central issue in social work, rather than being added as an afterthought.

White social workers will feel threatened by being placed in the unusual position of being judged by their black colleagues and will feel vulnerable when their work is found wanting. Thus it is important that employing authorities provide appropriate supervision and support to allow them to explore their anxieties, resolve the issues entailed in their role reversal, and ensure they become motivated into improving their work instead of wallowing in a morass of guilt and paralysis. Group supervision based on consciousness-raising techniques can move white social workers out of the trap of becoming pathologised as racist individuals. Similarly, white social work educators whose work is criticised from a black perspective will need support in improving the quality of their teaching.

The improvement of services for black people has positive implications for enhancing services more generally. For example, the Black Families Unit's critique of fostering arrangements has challenged both the criteria white social workers use in determining which families are suitable as foster parents and Lambeth's social services department's relationship with the black community as a whole, including the ways in which it informs black people and encourages their use of services available. Rating Lambeth's practices unsatisfactory on both counts, the Black Families Unit has revealed that black families were excluded from consideration by the white middle-class heterosexual norms which were used to judge them, and which underpinned the procedures used in communicating with them. In challenging the set-up for black families, black social workers have also exposed the systematic exclusion of white working class families, single parent families, and homosexual people for failing to conform to white middle-class heterosexist criteria of having large homes, a comfortable income and a stable, traditional family life. Following their analysis, black social workers have exerted pressure to make the department more responsive to the needs and life-styles of all the people it purports to serve. Thus the Black Families Unit has improved fostering service for white children as well as black children. White social work educators need to familiarise themselves with the work of such autonomous black groups and include them as an integral part of the social work curriculum, challenging in consequence the anglocentric nature of their teaching, and offering models of good social work practice endorsed by black people.

Moreover, autonomous black organisations enable black people to examine their position with their specific needs in mind without having these subsumed by those of others. Phillips (1982) argues that the Left, for example, continually subsumes black working-class people's needs under those of the white working class in theory and practice by maintaining that economic issues have priority over all others. Its stance negates the significance of race. Or, in Stuart Hall's words, such analyses 'ignore capitalist dynamics, for capitalism reproduces the working class in a racially stratified and internally antagonist form' (Hall, 1978, p.346). Similarly, black feminists argue white feminists subsume their specific interests under the notion of sisterhood. Yet their experience is not the same. White women enjoy power and privileges accruing to them as white women, but denied to black women (Carby, 1982; Hooks, 1981; Lorde, 1984; Parmar, 1982). For example, white women's right to have families is not questioned, though their right to control their sexuality and fertility is. But, as black feminists pointed out during the National Abortion Campaign, black women's right to a family and sexual expression is constantly being questioned by white people. They are forced into unwanted abortions and sterilisations because white doctors believe they should control their 'rampant fecundity' (Hooks, 1981). The immigration system persists in dividing black families, thereby enshrining the denial of their right to familyhood in a respectable institutionalised form. Parmar (1982) and Lorde (1984) also highlight the heterosexism in both black and white communities and argue strongly for the recognition of the specific forms of oppression black lesbians endure.

Changing directions in the social work curriculum

Altering the social work curriculum in anti-racist/non-racist directions means removing its anglocentric basis and arrogance to affirm black people in terms they define and present. Shifting the social work curriculum's political bias away from favouring the status quo towards one securing justice for oppressed groups will accord priority to social work's traditional caring values rather than its controlling ones. Ultimately, an anti-racist curriculum lays the foundations for a new type of social work – one that is not simply casework-oriented, although it will still deal with individual difficulties and suffering, but one which challenges structural constraints whilst simultaneously incorporating the dictum 'the personal is political', i.e. our individual experiences reflect the social position within which we find ourselves. Egalitarian relations acknowledging power differentials and the different life experiences between individuals and groups will have to be included in the format of the redefined social work task whether white social workers are working in one-to-one counselling, or with groups, or through community action and organisational change with either black or white people.

Changing the social work curriculum is only one of a number of changes which social work education must initiate. This has got to be combined with changes within CCETSW and its governing council. CCETSW's regulations governing social work education and training must foster anti-racist objectives. It should respond positively to demands for change being articulated by both black and white people, e.g. the Mickleton Group, and the White Collective for Anti-Racist Social Work. Black people must enter CCETSW's structures in significant numbers so that they can be empowered as a group rather than being individualised token solutions to institutionalised racism. Social work courses themselves need to attract black students and black teachers in substantial numbers so that they do not become isolated examples of white benevolence. CCETSW and central government must release sufficient resources to ensure anti-racism is handled appropriately. These resources need to cover more grants for black students, additional funding for recruiting black staff in educational institutions and the field, further in-service training money for existing white teaching staff and practitioners. Also, CCETSW must ensure anti-racist social work is assessed in its qualifying programmes in both written and placement work by making working in anti-racist ways a requirement for the satisfactory completion of courses. The requirement that students work along anti-racist lines would make anti-racist teaching mandatory.

The employment of teaching staff with a black perspective

Besides the racism evident in the recruitment and selection of students, course content, and practice placements, educational institutions embrace racist employment practices. Black supervisors and lecturers are under-represented on courses. Experienced black practitioners are often drafted in on poor conditions of employment as sessional teachers, filling gaps left by white colleagues rather than being employed on career grades with mainstream terms and conditions of work. White trainers have a significant role to play in reversing this situation by promoting organisational change in employment policies and practices.

To address the issue of providing students with more than an anti-racist reading list, white social work educators have to acknowledge that there are teaching processes which are beyond their expertise. White lecturers' limitations in teaching anti-racist social work include being unable to substitute for black people in giving white students experience of working with black teachers having the power to evaluate their achievements. White tutors cannot provide black students with either positive role models of black people, or the skills necessary for survival in a racist society. Neither can white educators form black support networks with black students. Consequently, courses lacking staff with a black perspective seriously handicap all students. White educators must, therefore, confront the thorny question of providing black and white students with the experience of working in an environment where black people occupy positions of authority (Dominelli, 1979).

In acknowledging openly their inability to provide black and white students with the full range of required educational services, white teachers can pave the way for the employment of black academic staff. White educators may perceive this suggestion as reinforcing competitive and conflictual relationships between black and white persons applying for the same jobs. As a number of them have said in discussions with me: 'I am not prepared to give up my job for a black person. I have my mortgage and my family to think about.' Such definitions of the problem are misleading. White anti-racist social work educators facing this analysis have to redefine the situation to clarify the nature of the issues being addressed. The discussion above reveals that the designation of white teachers as 'race experts' disguises the absence of black teachers for undertaking essential anti-racist teaching which cannot be provided by white tutors. Thus work currently undertaken by white educators and that which should be being done by black people is not conflictual, but complementary.

Individual white social work tutors concerned about the failure of courses to address the question of racism in social work, have placed themselves in a competitive relationship with black teachers by trying to provide *all* the 'anti-racist' teaching in the absence of black colleagues. Their single-handed attempts to challenge racism have confounded anti-racist practice, for, having little training in fighting the myriad manifestations of racism, white trainers unwittingly perpetuate racist practices in their establishments. The trap they unhappily embrace in becoming 'race relations experts' overnight is speaking on behalf of black people whose voice is either unheard by white people or absent physically and metaphorically from courses.

With declining funding, the well-meaning intentions of white social work educators have been unintentionally subverted by institutions which have found their white employees' willingness to act as 'race experts' an easy solution to the problem of inadequate resourcing for tackling racism. Instead of employing additional black staff to bring a black perspective into the work, institutions redeploy existing white staff without due regard either to what is required in anti-racist teaching or to the ability of white staff to undertake the whole range of such teaching. By covering gaps in service provisions through this process, institutions have exploited their white personnel, abused their humanity, and turned their professional ethics of meeting students' needs against them. In acquiescing to this, white tutors have personally colluded with institutionalised racism. Once embarked upon this process, feelings of powerlessness and isolation within their institutions have made it difficult for white educators and practitioners to individually resist pressures for their continued involvement. Black people's critique of their work has made white trainers realise just how their humanity and generosity has been hijacked by racist policies and practices which have kept black people out of academe (Dominelli, 1987).

Moreover, the more junior members of staff whose teaching is marginalised are more likely to have their humanity so compromised. The following examples illustrate the typical processes and situations replicated throughout Britain. In one university department, a white woman lecturer, appointed to teach community work, became appalled at the course's failure to address racism and initiated an option on it. Attempts to make racism a more central issue on the course where thwarted by cries of ,'We already have an overburdened timetable, we can't add more to it.' These objections were strengthened by the lack of resourcing within the department. This point was articulated as, 'We have no black members of staff and no money with which to appoint any.' Returning from a prolonged absence, the lecturer discovered her teaching had been restructured. Her normal areas of teaching had been dropped whilst her 'race options' teaching had been increased. Despite protests from the lecturer, this situation remained and the staff group congratulated themselves on 'doing as much as they could do given the circumstances'. In another university, a newly-appointed white male research-worker complained about the absence of teaching on racism in the social work course and was given the task of offering students an option on it. His pleas for the appointment of black staff went unheeded. Although polytechnics are currently leading universities in their preparedness to appoint black members of staff, their record in abusing white staff is equally poor. For instance, in one polytechnic, a white woman lecturer teaching mainly community work made it her responsibility to foster teaching on ethnic minorities in the department. As a result of her concern, she was forced to adopt the mantle of 'race expert' for 10 years before being able to convince her colleagues that they should be pushing their 'equal opportunities' employer to appoint their first black lecturer.

The abuse of white staff in this manner by employing authorities must end. CCETSW has a role in putting pressure on educational establishments to appoint black staff and helping them acquire the financial resources necessary for realising this objective. White educators can themselves take an initiative on this by organising collectively to expose the nature of the problem confronting them, and by collectively refusing to continue being used as 'race experts', empower themselves in challenging the exploitation of their labour. Redefining the problem to be confronted as institutionalised racism, i.e. employing authorities' failure to demand anti-racist teaching and practice from all existing staff and employ substantial numbers of black staff, can be very liberating for white educators and practitioners. Besides exposing employers' insistence that they undertake work which it is impossible for them to do, redefining the problem stops white practitioners and educators feeling guilty about attempting to work in 'anti-racist' ways and failing, thereby strengthening their resolve not to accept the label of 'race expert'. Moreover, once they see clearly the issues at stake, white social work educators and practitioners will be convinced to take action, not as individuals who can easily be picked off through allegations of breach of contract, but as a group of concerned professionals acting in concert to effectively resist being abused by their employers. Through collective action, their individual plight of feeling compelled by their institutions and their personal consciences to teach the impossible, will be both resisted and made visible in an extremely powerful way. Moreover, by organising collectively through their unions, professional organisations, and anti-racist support networks they would become pivotal in securing much needed changes in employment policies and practice.

Anti-racist practice placements: the anti-racist apprenticeship model

Training does not prepare white students for becoming anti-racist practitioners in an ethnically diverse society. They are seldom encouraged to confront racism in their practice placements and have their performance in doing so evaluated. If white students are in an office having neither black workers nor black people using its services, the fact is either ignored or interpreted as a comforting validation of the irrelevance of the personal social services to black people. White students are not required to work under the tutelage of black supervisors to experience directly a situation in which black people occupying powerful positions help them unravel their prejudices about black people's social status.

As white students are being trained to practice anywhere in Britain, and with all client groups, anti-racist practice ought to be a central feature of all placement work, whether or not black people are directly involved in the agency. Since challenging their stereotypes about black people and their role in society is an essential part of the anti-racist social work curriculum, all white students should have the opportunity of working under black fieldwork supervisors. This would help them acquire the skills of working in anti-racist ways and gain the cultural and ethnic sensitivity they need to work with black colleagues on an equal basis once they become paid employees. Their placement practice would also prepare them for intervening more appropriately and relevantly in their subsequent work with black people. The possibility of white students having direct experience of working under and being evaluated by black practitioners constitutes what I have called the 'anti-racist apprenticeship model' of teaching.

The suggestion that white students' practice placement be influenced and assessed by black practitioners should not be used either to 'dump' the responsibility for teaching anti-racist social work onto their shoulders, or to deny black students access to them. Black students also need black practitioners, but for different reasons – as positive role models and to help them acquire the skills they need to work in the racially uncongenial environment of social work. That both groups of students require black practitioners to complete their educational experience underlines the importance of drawing substantial numbers of black people into these positions.

For the opportunities in the 'anti-racist apprenticeship model' of teaching to be made available to white students, several changes have to take place in current practice. These include the large-scale employment of black people as practitioners in mainstream activities, counting student supervision in the normal workload of black workers, and providing them with the time and resources necessary for carrying out this work effectively. Universities and colleges would have to develop extensive links with black communities to ensure that they drew substantial proportions of academic staff and practitioners from these. Moreover, social work authorities and educational establishments as a group would have to put pressure on CCETSW to get it to change its requirements concerning the recognition of practice teachers and eliminate one obstacle to their recruitment – that all practice teachers be formally qualified and have two years of post-qualifying experience. This requirement discriminates indirectly against black people because it does not recognise experiences and qualifications obtained in countries other than Britain; does not accept that black people acquire their experience in the voluntary sector amongst black community groups whose concept of social work does not necessarily match that depicted in mainstream white agencies and endorsed by CCETSW; and does not acknowledge the institutionalised racism in education (Stone, 1981; ALTARF, 1984) which denies black people the opportunity to acquire the qualifications and experience demanded by CCETSW. Finally, CCETSW should endorse working in anti-racist ways by making it a compulsory aspect of placement assessment.

Black students and social work training

Black students' specific needs are virtually ignored in social work training. Few resources are earmarked specifically for them (Willis, 1987). Black students experience considerable discrimination in getting accepted onto social work courses; recruitment and selection procedures work against them (CCETSW, 1985). Their experience of working in black self-help groups is devalued and downgraded because it is different from that obtained in social services departments or probation offices. Considering only the experience gained in mainstream or statutory agencies as *real practice* reinforces racist definitions of social work. Black people working in unpaid capacities in voluntary agencies using a variety of social work techniques are also doing social work. Black people seldom sit on the interviewing panels making decisions about admissions to courses. This means white definitions of what constitutes social work practice go unchallenged in the interviewing process and black candidates are rejected as having 'unsuitable practice experience'. White candidates find their racist definitions of social work unquestioned and their commitment to working in anti-racist ways inadequately checked out. Rules regulating the funding of courses, especially those concerning secondment and discretionary grants also operate to the detriment of black applicants (Duffield, 1985). Mechanisms geared towards getting black students together as a group so that they can offer one another support against the racist practices that impinge daily in their lives as students are also missing on courses. The lack of black tutors in educational establishments denies black students access to positive models of black people working in authoritative positions. They also do not receive the support they need in discussing the problems of black people living in a racist society and in considering their position as black students with those in authority who have also experienced racist courses and survived. Furthermore, having black tutors enables black students to receive support in challenging racism on courses, e.g. assessment criteria which discriminate against them – an issue raised by black students at Bristol Polytechnic. Support networks of this form are crucial in challenging a trend towards disproportionately high failure rates among black students (Willis, 1987). In addition, few practice placements allow black students to work with black people under the supervision of black practitioners so that they can explore fully questions relating to their needs as black workers in a predominately white society. Nor do they get black supervisors to help them deal with the racism they encounter from white clients and white colleagues. The appointment of black staff would also help pre-empt the ghettoisation of black students as the 'experts' dealing with all the issues concerning 'race' on their courses.

Guidelines for white educationalists

This chapter has highlighted the weaknesses of social work education and training in fighting racist policies and practices. It has identified the need for white social work educators to come together collectively as a group and commit themselves to anti-racist social work in fairly practical ways. These can be summarised as follows:

1. developing an anti-racist social work curriculum aiming to replace anglocentric concepts in social work theory, practice, law, and policies with anti-racist ones;
2. transforming current definitions of what constitutes social work;
3. changing course selection and recruitment procedures so that only white people committed to anti-racist social work are admitted;
4. having selection panels which include black people who can ensure that non-racist definitions of social work are used in evaluating the suitability of black applicants for courses;
5. having recruitment and publicity materials geared towards encouraging black people to apply for courses;
6. employing a substantial proportion of black academic staff, administrative staff, and practitioners;
7. developing links with black communities to provide a substantial pool of placements through which black practitioners can evaluate the competence of students working with black people;
8. providing black students with the space and resources to develop autonomously as black students;
9. challenging CCETSW's current assessment criteria and replacing these with enforceable anti-racist ones;

10. demanding central government releases resources to employ black people throughout social work education and retrain white people already within it;
11. challenging institutionalised racism more generally by making explicit the gains accruing to white people by virtue of its existence and incorporating the exposure of these in their teaching;
12. getting white social work educators and practitioners to refuse to accept roles as 'race experts' who can offer black and white students the teaching and skills which can only emanate from a black perspective; and
13. making a commitment to working and teaching in anti-racist ways a criteria of employment in social work education.

3

Deconstructing Racism: Anti-Racism Awareness Training and Social Workers

Conscientisation (Freire, 1970), or the process whereby individuals make connections between the social relations they endorse and perpetuate through their attitudes, values and behaviour and the social positions they occupy, is an essential feature of anti-racist social work. But because white people's innermost concepts of positive selfhood can be exposed as illusory, becoming conscious or aware of the processes whereby they personally collude with institutional racism can be extremely uncomfortable and dispiriting, until they grasp the action enabling them to change the situation for the better. However, the means whereby white people, as the beneficiaries of white supremacy, embark on this process are not so easy to discern. The complexity of the enterprise makes it easy for white people to collude with one another and avoid confronting racist practices directly. White people use a variety of strategies drawing upon institutionalised racist norms, policies and practices and link these with their personal ones to facilitate their not facing the issues raised in eradicating racism. By perpetuating individual, institutional and cultural racism, these strategies work against the establishment of anti-racist social work. These may be identified as follows:

1. *Denial*. The refusal to accept racism, especially its cultural and institutional forms, exists. People using this strategy think of racism as personal prejudices held by a few extreme and irrational individuals.

71

2. *Omission*. The racial dimension of social interaction is ignored. Individuals subscribing to this view do not see the relevance of race in most situations, and relate to others as if racism did not exist.
3. *Decontextualisation*. Persons decontextualising racism accept that it exists in general terms, 'out there', e.g. in South Africa. But they refuse to believe it permeates the everyday activities they undertake.
4. *The colour-blind approach*. Black people are treated as if they were the same as whites. People holding this position negate black people's specific experience of racism in Britain.
5. *The 'dumping' approach*. The responsibility for creating racism and getting rid of it is placed on black people. Individuals acting on this basis blame the victims for what happens. Thus black people are held responsible for racism.
6. *The patronising approach*. White ways are deemed superior, but black people's ways of doing things are tolerated. Black people are considered entitled to their 'quaint ways'.
7. *Avoidance*. There is an awareness of 'race' as a factor in social interaction, but opportunities for confronting it are avoided. This usually means flinching at racist behaviour but keeping quiet about it.

Unearthing the ways in which these strategies prevent white people from initiating and realising anti-racist action is the aim of anti-racism awareness training. Anti-racism awareness awareness training is geared specifically at raising white people's consciousness of racism in all its manifestations and at helping them define and then undertake action aimed at countering these. Anti-racism awareness training is not necessary for black people. Assertion training is more relevant to their needs. Exploring the strategies whereby white people avoid challenging racism, the implications of this for social work practice, and the role anti-racism awareness training can play in tackling racism is the objective of this chapter.

Anti-racism awareness training is not predicated on a personal quest assuming individuals are free from their structural constraints as state employees. Anti-racism awareness training connects the individual, organisational and structural elements of social interaction. Taking changing the system as its central point, anti-racism awareness training attempts to deconstruct racism by demonstrating how personal change affected through increased consciousness of what one does as an individual fits into organisational and societal policies and practices. Besides making connections, anti-racism awareness training helps individuals acquire confidence in 'owning' or becoming accountable for their own actions. Individual behaviour is presented as having some autonomy from what happens in an organisation or society without being divorced from it. The ability of social workers to put themselves into their own social context is as important as their being able to place clients in their social setting. *Know thyself* is an important precept for white social workers to apply to their own racism. By understanding themselves, their value system, prejudices, position in society and the privileges accruing to them through racist social relations, white social workers can become racially aware in a manner which incorporates both the structural and the personal components of racism, raises their political consciousness of racial issues and rids them personally of racial prejudice, whether intended or not.

Embarking on a process of self-discovery enables white social workers undertaking anti-racism awareness training to examine the real extent of their racial tolerance instead of assuming it, and to unearth the white supremacy firmly entrenched within their alleged liberality. Discovering this makes white people uncomfortable, so they willingly collude with strategies camouflaging this unpleasant reality. This is illustrated in the comments made by a white person employing black trainers to run anti-racism training courses for white social work educators and practitioners:

Racism Awareness Training is a sensitive area. Many white people have had a bad experience of it, and so we have to consider carefully who we bring in to take charge of these courses. Originally, I agreed to go along with black trainers being bought in to do this teaching. I wanted someone who was good, but who would be sensitive to and careful with our feelings. I didn't want an 'uppity black' to take control of the thing.

Notions of white supremacy and commitment to having white people define the basis on which black people are employed are obvious from this account. There are other situations in which white people's beliefs in the correctness of having status, power and control are more subtly expressed. The subtlety of the dynamics involved came across when I used an exercise to explore the views of people who did not consider themselves racist. Those of you who feel this applies to you should undertake the following exercise and consider your answers in relation to those that came up in groups I have run:

A. *Write down your reasons for thinking you are not racist.*

B. *Then examine your answers in the light of the following questions*:

   a. How many dwelt solely on your personal attributes, i.e. failed to contextualise your views in structural terms taking account of your position as a white person in a predominantly white society?
   b. Have you identified those forces and relationships conferring power on you and those making you feel powerless?
   c. To what extent did you think about black people's experiences?

Most white respondents do not identify themselves as white, taking our white identity for granted as part of the privilege of belonging to the dominant group (Fletchman-Smith, 1984). If your replies indicate that you have taken your position as a 'white' person for granted, you are presupposing white supremacy. This is racist. Whilst white people can ignore their racial origins, black people are not allowed to forget theirs. The colour of their skin becomes the initial basis on which white people react to them. White social workers ignoring the significance of race for black people in their intervention are denying a crucial aspect of their existence, thereby creating a major obstacle to effective social work with them (Gitterman and Schaeffer, 1972). Moreover, white people relate to black people as *black* people, who are expected to behave in certain deferential ways and occupy inferior positions in the socio-economic hierarchy. Not taking such dynamics into account means white social workers are reinforcing racism by decontextualising black people. White people may have the luxury of forgetting that they are black; black people themselves do not (Riley, 1985).

White people also provide a catalogue of anti-racist activities, particularly campaigns in which they participate, to demonstrate their lack of racism. This suggests racism has nothing to do with them personally. Whilst supporting anti-racist activities alongside others, white people must tackle the ways in which their own day-to-day behaviour affirms institutionalised racism. Anti-racist social work does not separate the two, for institutional racism buttresses personal behaviour and personal behaviour feeds off institutional and cultural racism. Rather, it clarifies the interconnectedness between these three dimensions.

Becoming racially aware as individuals is essential for white social workers countering both institutionalised racism and racial prejudice amongst the broader public they meet during the course of their work. The objective of becoming racially aware can be achieved by engaging in a process combining anti-racist struggles with anti-racism awareness training. This message may strike readers as overtly political. It is. But all social work is political, regardless of the perspective from which it is practiced, because all social workers make decisions affecting other people's lives, and have the power to allow or deny people access to social resources. Social workers making these decisions within the parameters of the dominant ideology are not acting apolitically, they are reinforcing the *status quo* (see Lorde, 1984). The fact that decisions predicated on this basis are less likely to be questioned than those emanating from a perspective challenging established practice should not obscure the political nature of such acts. In a racist society, it is all to easy for white social workers to remain oblivious to the racist nature of their intervention. For unless they are racially aware, both they and their white colleagues will be colluding with racist policies and practices through their shared ideology of white supremacy.

Ignorance of what constitutes racist practice is not a valid justification for its perpetuation. Every white social worker practising in an ethnically pluralist society is morally as well as socially obliged to raise their consciousness and take personal and organisational steps to eradicate racist practice. Racist practices are those actions, decisions and policies which either directly or indirectly ascribe an inferior status to black people and deny ethnic or racial groups access to their share of society's power, resources and dignity. In social work this includes the failure of service delivery to meet the specific needs of ethnic minority groups, to provide employment and training opportunities commensurate with their numbers in the population at large and to validate black people's resistance to oppression.

Furthermore, in a climate of public expenditure cuts state attempts to ration social services resources intensify pressure on social workers to act as agents of social control reducing demands for scarce public resources. The high visibility of certain ethnic groups, particularly black ones, makes it easier for them to be targeted as objects whose eligibility to services must be authenticated above and beyond 'normal' standards. This is usually achieved by white professionals demanding that black people produce their passports before being given access to services. The possibility that these Asian families may be black British, and therefore wholly entitled to the services available under the welfare state is submerged by white social workers' anxiety that they are dealing with 'immigrants'. It is a racist position which gives black people the loud and clear message that they have not really been accepted as having a rightful place in Britain.

Anti-racism awareness training

Anti-racism awareness training must become an integral part of social work education and in-service training so that white social workers can pick up on their internalised racism and the myriad ways in which their social interaction utilises racist behaviour to denigrate black people during teacher–student, practitioner–student, social worker–client, and worker–worker relationships. Becoming racially aware is not an exercise in guilt expiation, but a first step in developing anti-racist practice. It proceeds through consciousness-raising, making individuals aware of the connections between personal, institutional and cultural racism, and their operation and reinforcement through everyday actions and attitudes. The next stage concerns the individual making a commitment to struggling against racism knowing that the process may well be painful, and developing strategies of action for combating racism individually and collectively. Having worked these out, the individual embarks on implementing the action. This section contains exercises exploring white social workers' racist assumptions, helping them become more racially aware in the process.

I draw a distinction between race awareness training, racism awareness training and anti-racism awareness training. Although only one part of it, language is an important aspect of the oppression process (Spender, 1980). *Race awareness training* becomes problematic because it defines 'race' as the problem to be tackled. This sidetracks us down the path of biological determinism searching for a mythical black race and mythical white one, whereas we have seen 'race' is a social construct imbedded in all aspects of human relations. *Racism awareness training* in defining racism as the problem to be addressed, focuses on the social processes and the power differentials existing between different ethnic minority groups. *Anti-racism awareness training* goes one step further to legitimate combining action aimed at eradicating racism with an appreciation of its effects. Hence I believe we should shift from race awareness and racism awareness training to anti-racism awareness training.

Race awareness training developed in the aftermath of black criticism of white involvement in the Civil Rights Movement in the USA. White liberals became perplexed when black militants accused them of being racist and of becoming involved in anti-racist struggles to assuage their feelings of guilt and complicity rather than to liberate black people (Cleaver, 1971). As the black critique increased in strength and popularity in black communities, black-only organisations replaced mixed ones and white progressives were left out in the cold, feeling confused by the message given by those whose aspirations they endorsed (Adamson and Borgos, 1985).

Some 'progressive' whites have interpreted black people's call as one requiring them to do nothing since fighting racism is the prerogative of black activists. Others have felt discomfited by this interpretation and have probed deeper to find a significant role for themselves in the struggle against racism. The central message black people have given progressive white people is that we are so conditioned by living in a racist society and so imbued with the privileges stemming from it, we cannot see either our own racism, or the benefits accruing to us because of its existence, or our role in perpetuating it. Although we use race in a highly politicised way, we are racially blind when looking at ourselves and our behaviour.

Moreover, black people's own consciousness and sense of self-worth had reached the stage where they were no longer prepared to tolerate white patronage, condescension and paternalism, whether it was well-intentioned or not (Cleaver, 1971). Standing up against white liberal intentions of 'doing good' is essential for black people's own social growth and development, and for reclaiming their self-respect. Their taking this stand is crucial in steering white progressives into anti-racist directions, and compelling them to focus their energies on white racism.

White progressives culling this message from black people's rejection of their earlier contribution to the anti-racist struggle have turned to examining themselves and the social relationships mediating their interaction with blacks. This exercise has unearthed the material basis for black people's allegations. The complexity of the project white people are embracing and the myriad subtle ways in which racism operates and is perpetuated have been quickly realised. The attempt to become racially aware has brought humility amongst white progressives who now wonder at their earlier arrogance in thinking they had all the answers. As one practitioner on an anti-racism awareness training course said to me, 'Humility and the realisation that I'm not so superior is what I take from this.' White social workers need to make humility part of their willingness to listen to black clients and learn to treat seriously their view of a situation. This awareness must be coupled with using the power they wield as white social workers to undertake anti-racist action.

There is a paradox in this position, for the power for white social workers to decide to accept the anti-racist struggle remains with them. But this is consistent with white people accepting the notion that racism is their problem and taking responsibility for dismantling the racist edifice which they have created. In assuming responsibility for their actions, white people can enact human intentionality, take control of events, and ensure that they unfold along liberating lines, that is, those endorsing racial equality and justice.

Judy Katz's book, *White Awareness*, was amongst the first American publications in the race awareness training field, and has contributed considerably to its discussion in Britain. Though race awareness training here is in its early days, Katz' contribution has been critiqued by those attempting to transcend the limitations of her pioneering efforts. Gurnah (1984) criticises racism awareness training, including Katz' seminal work, for diverting the energies of black activists; being colonised by the state, which uses racism awareness training courses to give an illusion of tackling racism when it is giving priority to controlling both black and white opposition to it; lacking a clearly articulated theoretical analysis of racism; failing to initiate change which would benefit black communities; and reducing racism to an abstract entity contained within the person. To this list, I would add further reservations. These are: a) a naive view of power; b) a failure to root racism within patriarchal capitalist society, although Katz acknowledges racism occurs within a social context; c) an end product of paralysing guilt rather than a spur to action; and d) an over-emphasis on what *individuals* can or must do.

I draw a deeper distinction than Katz (1978) between racial prejudice and racism – individuals hold racial prejudice, but it requires the exercise of power to make it racism. I share Katz' definition of racism to a point. But in my view *all* white individuals in Britain exercise some power over black individuals by virtue of their being *white* people in a predominately *white* society. Even in one-to-one interactions between black and white, that power balance hangs in the air by an invisible cord, and shifts in favour of the white person. Hence, I would argue that in a white capitalist society all racial prejudice is tinged with racism to varying degrees. By becoming aware of this factor, white social workers developing anti-racist practice can take it into account in their work with black clients.

Power relationships predicated on membership of the white community are reflected in the assumptions white social workers make about black clients. These include the belief that black people are recent immigrants. Yet black people have been settling in Britain for over 500 years (Fryer, 1984). Furthermore, 40 per cent of black people are Black British people born here. Thus when white social workers ask black children they are placing in a nursery, 'Which part of India are you from?', the message being conveyed to them is, 'You don't belong here. You are not one of us'. Underpinning this statement is the view that the black person is not entitled to this service (or can only have it on sufferance). The message is a racist one.

And when such messages are communicated in a climate endorsing repatriation for black people, they exacerbate a racist situation. That white social workers intend to welcome black people into a white milieu through such statements does not make vulnerable individuals feel less anxious, if this is the nature of their initial greeting. White social workers facing such predicaments should give priority to establishing their friendliness and commitment to fighting racism by ensuring that the appropriate services are made available to them. Questions of origins can be asked later when a climate of safety and trust prevails. White social workers should then feel able to reveal their ethnic origins and talk about these too. Being open about their own racial and ethnic identity can empower white social workers. Recovering the positive aspects of Anglo-Saxon ethnicity, e.g. its collectivism via extended kinship and community ties can be a vital step in the process of reclaiming their humanity.

The emphasis on individual racism in both race awareness and racism awareness training is problematic in terms of the processes in which they lock white participants. Their individualistic approach emphasises the need to resolve personal hang-ups about racism and hinders the realisation of the collective responsibility white people have in eradicating racism as a system. This has led to conflicts between white people newly arrived to the issue wanting to concentrate on discovering what 'racism' is, and those having worked on this aspect for some time pushing themselves and others into developing strategies for structural change. The frustrations present between them pit white individuals who are at different starting points in the conscientisation process against one another. White participants come to race awareness and racism awareness training courses already divided by a number of hierarchies including employment status and gender – features which race awareness and racism awareness training set aside as diversions allowing white people to avoid the task of confronting racism. These divisions result in white people competing with one another to establish who is the least racist of the lot, thereby exacerbating the divisions between them and setting in train rivalries which are destructive to collaborative work aimed at fighting racism. These rivalries feed on individual fears and insecurities sparked off when their self-concepts as non-racists have been undermined and challenged. These fears immobilise white people through the guilt and shame they feel having exposed undesirable facets of their behaviour without replacing these with desirable ones. Others are paralysed by their fear of challenging authorities on which their livelihood depends. Others are incapacitated by race awareness and racism awareness training's insistence that they bare their feelings. Some are frustrated by their failure to make the links between personal awareness and social action.

Anti-racism awareness training tries to grapple with these differences directly by establishing relations based on acknowledging and respecting the *different social positions* occupied by different groups of people and undertaking steps to reduce power differentials between them. Only when this has happened will real social change affecting the individual and society take place (Lorde, 1984). Anti-racism awareness training takes these dynamics on board, not necessarily by addressing each one specifically, but by focusing white people's energies on achieving personal change by transforming those systems in which they find themselves. This process commences with a redefinition of the problem away from individual pathology and onto inadequate social structures and oppressive social relations and taking action against these.

Anti-racism awareness training starts from the premise that society's social organisation is responsible for creating racism and that individuals perpetuate it in their actions because the social relationships they enact reproduce racist structures and patterns of behaviour. Hence individuals are crucial in perpetrating racism, but racism transcends their individual actions and behaviour. That our social organisation creates and legitimates racism does not absolve individuals from taking a stand against it. Social organisation is created by people. And people can change society if they have the will and collective organisation to direct towards dismantling society's racist bulwark and eliminating institutionalised racism. Bearing in mind that the forms racism assumes and our understanding of the steps necessary for its elimination vary over time as socio-economic conditions change, white social workers can become involved in the struggle to eradicate racism by: a) becoming racially aware individuals; b) working to eliminate institutionalised racism in their agency and in their practice; and c) taking up the anti-racist struggle more generally through political activity.

Exercises aimed at examining personal awareness of racism

The connections between individual racism and institutional and cultural racism can be explored by examining how these are embedded in our perceptions of black people and the statements we make about them in performing our daily work.

Exercise 1: Examining our views on who holds power

This exercise explores white social workers' unconscious endorsement of relations of subordination in their understanding of black people's location in the labour hierarchy and the status they hold.

A. Imagine yourself and your reactions in the following hypothetical situation:

> You are a white social worker and have been talking on the phone to the Head of a residential home about getting a place for one of your clients across a period of a couple of weeks. You eventually meet the person when you go to take the client there. You discover that person is black. (You can imagine yourself talking to any other highly placed person elsewhere if this facilitates your thinking about it.)

B. Then answer the following questions:

> a. Did you expect the Head of the home to be white?
> b. How did you react to the discovery that s/he was black?
> c. To what extent were you surprised to see a black person in charge?
> d. Why were you surprised (even if only ever so slightly)?

To understand the racism latent in this situation, we have to consider the responses ranging from a low degree to a high degree of surprise in terms of our assumptions and expectations about who holds power in society. The norm is that the powerholder is a white middle-class male. Our acceptance of this state of affairs as white social workers is revealed through: a) the surprise, albeit well-disguised, when we encounter black people in decision-making posts. This is particularly evident when a black person is in charge of a home with mainly white residents, or a district team in a predominantly white area; and b) not questioning the lack of black representation amongst fieldworker grades and in the upper echelons of the decision-making apparatuses.

White social workers' assumption that white people are the legitimate holders of society's resources is indirectly revealed when they express surprise that black clients have 'nice homes', 'nice cars', etc. Implied in these statements is the view that they have goods which are inappropriate for those in their place, i.e. 'they have risen above their station' (Comer, 1975). Such judgmental comments appear in social enquiry reports. Sometimes racist comments are made when attempting to counter racist expectations. The following example taken from a social enquiry report written by a white probation officer on a black man is indicative of this.

> The probation officer wrote, 'Mr K has a brand new Rover, which he paid for in cash.' Since Mr K had not been charged with stealing a Rover (or any other car), anti-racist social workers would question the relevance of this information. When asked, the probation officer concerned replied he wanted to pre-empt the court's expectations about Afro-Caribbeans. He thought showing Mr K's diligence might secure a more lenient treatment from the court. Mr K had been charged with assault. He claimed he had been defending himself from a racist attack by a group of white lads who were not facing charges.

This short extract exposes a number of racist stereotypes and assumptions revolving around black people's immigration status; black people's capacity to work and save money; black people's right to defend themselves against racist attack; and white privilege in defining the situation.

Exercise 2: Examining 'hidden' racism

White people's assumptions about and perceptions of black

people and the allocation of power and resources to them can be usefully explored in a group setting. The following exercise is aimed at doing this and can be undertaken in an area team. However, black members of the team should not participate in this exercise. Because of the hurtful nature of the statements, it is inappropriate to use them in helping their white colleagues deal with their racism. The statements should be read out and responses made initially in a *brainstorming session* format. A brainstorming session allows all participants to make spontaneous statements which are written down when they are made without being evaluated for merit. The responses are subsequently analysed and assessed by the group, highlighting the racist elements contained within them. The advantage of doing this exercise in a white group is that it allows individuals to appreciate the complexities of racism and compare their perceptions, attitudes and understanding of structural constraints with others.

The statements below reveal both the subtlety and variety of ways in which racism expresses itself in the actions and attitudes of social workers. And they show how these are underpinned by policies and practices which are racist in their effect. These statements, made by white social workers, form the basis of the brainstorming session.

Statements:

1. Black clients come to the office with so many conflicting demands. What do they *really* want?
2. Racism is rare amongst social workers.
3. Other ethnic minority groups have settled in Britain and improved themselves without 'positive discrimination'. Why shouldn't black people do likewise?
4. When black clients get angry, I feel so helpless.
5. The problem isn't racism. It's just that social workers don't feel good about themselves and what they are doing.
6. I'm not racist, I just think each ethnic group is different and should keep itself to itself. Black social workers should deal with black clients.
7. When a black client complains, hundreds of white

people rush in to help. If a white client complains, everyone turns deaf.

8. How can I be pro-black clients, without being anti-white clients?

9. I personally have no say in the formation of this Department's policies, racist or otherwise.

10. How can social workers solve *the black problem*?

11. Every individual client should be judged on his or her merits.

12. Black clients and community groups could do more for themselves by using the anti-racist legislation available in Britain.

13. Black clients should acknowledge social workers' efforts in dealing with the black problem. They are doing all they can to help.

14. I know these clients so well, I never think of them as black.

15. Some of my closest social work colleagues are black.

16. Black clients are over-sensitive. They over-react by reading more into a situation than is really there.

17. Home Office statistics have shown that there is a higher crime rate in black neighbourhoods.

18. For white social workers to progress in their anti-racist work, groups examining racism in their departments must include black members.

19. Black clients shouldn't be expected to integrate into British society if they don't really want to.

20. Black clients who show an interest in their affairs don't want us to deal with their problems.

Now examine your replies. You will discover that the statements cover racism in a number of different guises. The key ones which should be highlighted are the variety of ways in which black people are blamed for creating racism; holding black people responsible for eradicating racism; devaluing black people's contribution to society; pathologising black people and their culture; exaggerating the progress white people have made in eliminating racism; assuming white ways of doing things are superior; and, believing that race is not a crucial issue in Britain.

Although there are a number of aspects of racism which can be identified in each statement, the key ones are:

1. White people assume black people do not know what they want. It's a way of trivialising their demands and struggles for racial justice. White people from their superior standpoint do know.
2. Racism is defined as crude, irrational behaviour, thereby ignoring the significance of institutional and cultural racism on personal attitudes and action.
3. The person making the statement has failed to grasp the specific conditions surrounding the black experience of life in Britain. Structurally, it is not the same as earlier groups of settlers.
4. The statement blames the victims for their plight.
5. This comment attempts to avoid the issue.
6. Black people are held responsible for racism and for doing something about it. It suggests there is no role for white people in deconstructing racism.
7. The impact of anti-racist measures thus far is being exaggerated.
8. By assuming that black and white people are at the same starting points, and in competition with each other, the person is making inappropriate comparisons.
9. In externalising racism, such individuals are abrogating personal responsibility for what happens in a racist society, and denying their role in perpetuating racism.
10. This statement pathologises black people, and separates social work off from what happens in society, seeing it as an apolitical activity.
11. By looking at the situation in universalistic terms, the person is not recognising the specificity of the black experience. It is structurally different from that of whites.
12. Responsibility for eradicating racism is shunted onto black people's shoulders. It also ignores the weakness of the Race Relations Act in enforcing anti-racist measures.
13. This comment reveals how white people exaggerate their efforts and their impact in eliminating racism.
14. This statement depicts the *colour-blind* approach.

15. By treating black people as if they were white people, this comment is assimilationist. Black people with their specificity washed out are acceptable to white people who can make exceptions for the few who are not like the rest, i.e. *black*.
16. This statement blames the black victim.
17. The white person is pathologising black people.
18. In this comment white people shunt responsibility for eliminating racism onto black people.
19. By presenting racism as a matter of personal choice, this statement ignores the institutional and cultural dimensions of racism.
20. The responsibility for eliminating racism is placed upon black people.

Anti-racism awareness training and organisational change: changing employment policies

Black people's employment prospects in social work reflect institutionalised racism. They are generally employed in small numbers in the low status echelons of the labour hierarchy, particularly in residential work and on Section 11 contracts. Black people are largely absent from prestigious posts and the range of work. White people take this situation for granted, assuming black people are suitable only for a limited number of jobs. Anti-racism awareness training engages white social workers in organisational change opening up opportunities for black people. This they can undertake by confronting agency policy and practice in terms of a) the resources made available to black people; b) the employment of black workers within that agency; and c) the position of black people within the agency's decision-making structures. White social workers should look at their agency policies and practice and ask the following questions:

a. In which services are black people either under-represented or over-represented?
b. What are the reasons for their being either under-represented or over-represented?

c. How can either their under-representation or their over-representation be rectified so that racial justice and equality is ensured?
d. What positions do black people hold within this agency?
e. Are black people found proportionately at all levels of the agency's career ladder?
f. If black people are either absent as workers or dispor-portionately represented at the lowest rungs of the career ladder, what steps need to be taken to correct this?

The following exercise sensitises white social workers to some of the issues they will confront when undertaking organisational change. A fuller discussion of this takes place place in Chapter 5.

Exercise 3: Simulation/role play

You are a white social worker in Midletown District Team A. The area's housing stock is fairly run-down, employment opportunities are few. Middletown's population contains 15 per cent black people. The black population has been there for a very long time, and two-thirds of the young people under 30 were born in Middletown. They are descendants of people whose origins were in the Indian sub-continent, Africa, the Caribbean and China. Your team is located in the middle of an area inhabited mainly by blacks, but few of them come to you as clients. None of the workers in your team is black. There is, however, one black home-help, a Muslim woman born in the Gujerat in India. The cleaning lady was born in Jamaica. You have been on an anti-racism awareness training course and the extensive racism in the situation strikes you on return. You raise the matter informally with your colleagues, but they think you are exaggerating the matter. You discuss the problem with your senior during a supervision session and agree to discuss the issue in a team meeting. There are so many aspects you want to take up, you don't know where to begin. You decide it might be simplest if you tried arguing for the employment of a black social worker. Role-play your team meeting.

Take 10 minutes to assign roles and have individuals prepare themselves.

Characters: You can base the role-play on the following characters, or vary them to resemble your own team more closely if you wish:

District Manager: S/he tries to be helpful, but is fairly muddled in her/his thinking on this issue.

Principal Social Worker: Her/his main interest is in child abuse cases. S/he doesn't think much of this happens in black communities.

Home Help Organiser: S/he thinks s/he has 'done her/his bit' by having one black home-help already when there are few black elderly clients on the books. For this, s/he blames the social workers. Anyway, white people have complained when Mrs Kahn went to them. She kept coughing over everything.

Social Worker, Level 3: S/he doesn't think black people should be 'given' social work jobs. They should be properly qualified for them and get them in competition with others.

Social Worker, Level 2: S/he has much sympathy for your views, but doesn't see how the situation could be changed. S/he is the NALGO team representative.

Social Worker, Level 1: S/he came on the course with you and agrees with your analysis. S/he thinks you are 'brave' to try and do something about it.

Social Care Assistant: S/he thinks you are coming up with another of your 'new-fangled' ideas. You get one everytime you go on a course, but they never amount to much. Mind you, s/he's never seen you so 'het up' about things before.

Several Observers: To watch the role-play and take notes.

Duration of role-play: 20 minutes

Discussion: Guideline Questions. Take an hour for the discussion. Spend a few minutes after the role-play talking about how each person felt in his/her role. Then consider the following questions:

1. What aspects of each character in the role-play did you identify as racist?
2. What aspects of the organisation's policies and practices did you identify as racist?
3. What strategies can you develop for changing some of the attitudes and understandings of your colleagues?
4. How can you develop support for your ideas?
5. What measures can you take to stop yourself from feeling isolated, frustrated and bad about what is happening?
6. What organisations, groups and individuals could you contact to help you change agency policies and practices?
7. How can you get your union to adopt anti-racist policies?
8. How could you develop more appropriate relationships with the black communities on your doorstep, bearing in mind their heterogeneity?

Introducing organisational change is a difficult and challenging process, made even more problematic because those initiating change are simultaneously struggling with their own racist stereotypes and expectations. This becomes especially relevant in the treatment of the 'black community' as a homogeneous entity; and perceiving the employment of a few black workers as solving the problem of racism.

Anti-racist awareness training and trainers

The previous exercises show how difficult and complicated is the business of becoming racially aware and moving into anti-racist practice. Though not the ultimate word on the issue, they highlight how much work remains to be done to function appropriately as an anti-racist practitioner on the personal, interpersonal and organisational levels. I strongly recommend that all white social workers participate in anti-racism awareness training, bearing the following in mind. Firstly, anti-racist awareness training, if done properly will not be an easy undertaking for white social workers. It will profoundly challenge your concepts of self, of others, and your relationships with them. So, prepare yourself for an emotionally draining time. Secondly, the question of whom you should approach to do this work with you is not easily answered. There is considerable controversy about who should be involved in teaching on these courses and whether white trainers can perform an adequate job. I take the view that talking about the experience of black people is a matter that only they can address. Hence, only black trainers should be used in this context. However, there is a role for white trainers in talking about how we utilise racist practices to reproduce and perpetuate both individual, institutional and cultural racism; what racism does to us; asking questions about what we can do to carry on the anti-racist struggle in our organisations and amongst our colleagues; and considering the steps we need to take to achieve this. White trainers can also help develop support groups for white anti-racist social workers struggling with the resistance emanating from white colleagues and the exasperation of black colleagues for their failure to substantially progress their implementation of anti-racist practice.

4

Social Working Black Families

The white supremacist ideology deeply embedded in social work practice can be explored by examining white social workers' intervention in black families. The family, as the raw material of practice, provides the major backdrop against which social work intervention occurs. White feminists have criticised at length white social workers' involvement with white families (Wilson, 1977; Dominelli, 1986). But when it comes to intervening in black families, white social workers pretend there has been no such critique and that the white family, in contrast to the black family, is the source of all that is wonderful. Intervention in black families is problematic for white social workers because they treat black family forms as pathological and deviant for transmitting traditions differing from the white middle class heterosexual ones. As one white social worker involved with an Afro-Caribbean family informed me: 'They are not like us. They're more strict with their children. They're more ambitious for them.' Handling black families in these terms is racist. It enables white social workers to problematise black families by classifying their relationships, expressions of concern for each other's welfare, and childcare methods, inferior to white ones, and by labelling these inadequate and inappropriate (Mama, 1980) undermine the confidence of black parents and black children (Comer, 1975). Black people's aspirations for improvement in their status through upward mobility has been stigmatised as over-ambitious (Ahmed, 1984). Their rejection of the inferior status allo-

93

cated to them has been castigated by white social workers as poor socialisation for the roles they can occupy in Britain. As one white social worker put it: 'Asian families are not preparing children for the jobs they can take in society. They refuse to allow their youngsters to join YTS schemes preferring them to go on in school and train to be engineers!'

Black families are generally presented as breaking down and in crises by white people who do not see their dynamic presence and positive influence in black peoples' lives (Bromley, 1972). White social workers constantly belittle black families by pathologising them, seeing in them only weaknesses and ignoring their strengths. Yet black family forms have shown remarkable resilience, enabling black people to survive society's racist onslaughts upon them, and offering them a positive sense of identity which contrasts strongly with the negative one posited by white social workers (Bryan, 1985; Amos, 1984; Bromley, 1972). White social workers' pejorative assessment of black families and the reinforcement of racist stereotypes through their intervention are central to the 'social working', i.e. social control, of black families and form the major avenues through which they 'clientise' black people.

Thus the personal social services, like the educational system and the criminal justice system, reinforce racist stereotypes pathologising black people and confirming their subordinate status. The dynamics of pathology underpin the clientisation of black people. The clientisation of black people is the process whereby black people having 'client' status are systematically belittled, have their contribution to society devalued, and their access to their share of social resources including the personal social services blocked. Black people become 'clients' through referrals from welfare organisations including the health services, the agencies of law and order, and themselves.

The social working of black families by white social workers is particularly evident in their handling of child abuse in black families, fostering and adoption of black children, and issues affecting black women, black youth, and black elders. This chapter examines the ways in which white social workers pathologise black families through their interventions amongst these client groups.

The myth of the black family

White stereotypes of black families are rooted in social relations founded on arrogant and racist notions of white cultural supremacy. These begin with the idea that there is *one* black family type which acts as the norm whereby all black families are gauged. Except that 'the black family' exists in the perceptions of and is reinforced through the practices of white people, there is in reality, *not the black family, but a rich and diverse variety of black family forms* each with their own specific set of relationships, obligations and networks. The myth of 'the black family' has been given a significant measure of respectability and credence through academic works such as Moynihan's *The Negro Family*, which assembles 'facts' substantiating white people's stereotypes about black families. Although this book was quickly and thoroughly discredited by black authors (e.g. Ryan, 1965; Rainwater, 1966; Hill, 1972), it has entered the gates of academe to become a 'classical text' on 'the black family' in both Britain and America. The analysis that the black American family 'has been forced into a matriarchal structure which . . . seriously retards the progress of the group a a whole, and imposes a crushing burden on the Negro male and . . . Negro women' (Moynihan, 1965) confirms white people's view of black families as deviant and unstable. Usually used in teaching without reference to black writers' critiques, this book reproduces these myths in generations of young scholars who go on to become social workers and community activists.

Common stereotypes of the black family cover the sexual prowess of black men; the lack of sexual morality amongst black women as evidenced by a high ratio of single parenthood; the absence of a stable family tradition; the lack of family bonds between family members; and the power of strong, domineering matriarchs complemented by weak black men incapable of sustaining stable relationships (*Ebony*, 1985). These myths reveal that black families are being measured against the norm of the ideal, white middle-class heterosexual nuclear family.

These stereotypes negate the living reality of black people, but judge it in negative terms problematising 'the

black family'. White racism is more complex and contradictory than its myths on 'the black family' imply. As Amrit
Wilson demonstrates, sexism, racism and ignorance com-
bine to condemn black people whatever they do. For
example, a white male psychiatrist accused a young Bangladeshi woman he was allegedly treating for depression of
being morally 'loose' because she wore beautiful saris
(Wilson, 1978, p.24). Moreover, white British people draw
distinctions between the 'West Indian family' and the 'Asian
family'. Thinking of the range in family forms existing
amongst people whose origins are in the Caribbean Islands
and the Indian sub-continent in these terms creates sub-
divisions in the myth of 'the black family', turning the myth
on its head whilst still drawing on the stereotypes contained
within it. West Indian families are deemed unstable because
'they are run by domineering women who are morally
loose'. The strength and unity of the Asian family is
problematised. Asian women are too docile and sexually
repressed (Wilson, 1978). Asian men are too powerful.
From this we can conclude that whatever living arrangements black people make, white people will find them
wanting.

   White people ignore the fact that black people do not
have a right to family life (see Plummer, 1978). Immigration
controls since 1962 have made it virtually impossible for
black family units to exist in their totality in Britain, as the
following example demonstrates: A Pakistani Muslim man
was made redundant and sought advice from an Advice
Centre on making a claim for supplementary benefit. He
had two of his children living with him and his wife in
England. His other two children, one aged 12 and the other
aged 15, were living with relatives in Pakistan. Before
becoming unemployed, he used to send money to his
relatives for their care. Now, he was having problems
making ends meet. His wife did not get child benefit for
his two children resident outside Britain because this is
prohibited by the legislation governing entitlement to child
benefit. The welfare rights worker, a white man, felt unable
to offer the claimant any support for his claim. This case
exemplifies how white workers collude with institutionalised

racism. The white worker was placed in this position by the way his job was defined, i.e. giving advice on the existing legislation. Advice work predicated on responding to individual requests does not facilitate challenging the racist bases of its provisions. The white worker wanting to respond to the obvious needs of the black man in meeting his responsibilities to his dependents, felt powerless and hamstrung by the framework in which he operated. When telling me of his predicament, he said: 'There was nothing I felt I could do. I didn't know how to give him what he wanted. And, I'm not very good at challenging racism, though it was clear to me this was what I was up against.'

Had this white advice worker been working in anti-racist ways, taking on institutionalised racism would have been central to his response. To do this, he would have had to redefine his task and work simultaneously on several levels, drawing on the help of others – colleagues, his own organisation and people in other organisations. On the individual level, he would have sought to relieve the client's personal distress by facilitating contact between him and black organisations experienced in dealing with similar situations. Besides ensuring that the claimant was getting everything to which he was entitled, the advice worker could have investigated other sources for financial aid and helped him expedite his application to bring his children to Britain, by calling on other organisations and resources, e.g. Joint Council for the Welfare of Immigrants (JCWI) and United Kingdom Immigrants Advisory Service (UKIAS), various immigration campaigns, MPs, the CRE. Dealing with institutionalised racism in the child benefit legislation would have required the white worker to involve himself and others in a campaign exposing the injustices perpetrated by the existing provisions and putting pressure on the government to change the legislation on child benefits. Thus the white worker would have been challenging the view that the claimant was creating a problem by having his children in Pakistan, and focusing instead on an an iniquitous system.

Poor employment prospects and bad housing also deny black people choices in establishing their preferred family forms. White social workers continue to divide black families by taking disproportionate numbers of black children into care by 'inappropriately intervening in the family process' (Lambeth, 1981). Revealing that black children are more likely to end up in care than white children when white social workers intervene in their families, the Lambeth child care study exposes a further disturbing trend. Whilst white children in care come from families which are 'atypical' of the white families in the borough, black children come from families which are: 'very representative of black families in the borough, covering a wider range of income, employment and housing situations' (Lambeth, 1981, p.7). In other words, white social workers are pronouncing the whole spectrum of black families inadequate. The high-profile intervention white social workers adopt in reaction to black families reveals that although their intervention in general compels white families to stay together, it forces black families apart. It has led black people in Lambeth to perceive white social workers as child snatchers.

White social work intervention with black children

White social workers' anxieties about the appropriateness of black families' child-rearing practices, relationships between black parents and their children, and women's roles within black families, are central in the social work equation of pathologising black families. White supremacist values direct white social workers' thinking along the lines that black children are more appropriately either fostered and adopted by white families or brought up in predominantly white institutions. These have led to inappropriate forms of intervention and a poor service for the individuals concerned, e.g. not placing black children in care with black foster and adoptive families, failing to staff residential institutions with black employees at all levels, and not creating an anti-racist environment capable of nurturing black identity and psychological development in residential establishments. Meanwhile, white people congratulate themselves on doing a good job becuase 'the children suffered no obvious harm' (Gill and Jackson, 1982). This usually means black children have been successfully indoctrinated into thinking they are white (BCSG, 1986). That is, they have had to either repress or reject their black identity and become *colour-blind*, reflecting the nature of the white families into which they have been placed.

In keeping with their white cultural supremacist belief that white child-rearing practices are superior to black ones, white social workers resist the idea that black families can appropriately foster and adopt white children. Hence, they are reluctant to accept black parents as bona fide fosterers and adopters by placing white children in their homes. This traffic in children has been criticised by black practitioners for being one way: black children going into white foster homes (Small, 1987; ABSWAP, 1981; Devine, 1983). The lack of mutuality in the placing of children in care has caused black professionals to define such practices as another form of cultural imperialism in which black children become commodities of exchange (Comer, 1972; ABSWAP, 1981). Whether white people agree with this interpretation of the transaction is irrelevant. The important questions white social workers have to consider are why so few prospective black parents for fostering and adopting black children are on their books and why virtually no white children are placed with black families. White social workers who justify this situation by saying that children are best placed with those who share similar racial and cultural backgrounds still have to explain why this axiom does not apply to black children. An honest answer is better than one camouflaging racist practice for it at least allows organisations and individuals the possibility of undertaking action to reverse their position. White social workers attempting to blame black communities for the lack of black adoptive and fostering families also need to explain why authorities such as Lambeth acting under pressure from black social workers to alter their procedures and criteria for selecting black foster parents have few problems filling their books with potential black foster families (Small, 1987). The inclusion of other important criteria – the ability to love and relate to a black child as a *black child*, the skills in handling racist onslaughts, a sense of positive black identity — essential to the full development of black children did not take place until black practitioners criticised the previous criteria. Their challenge has yielded better practice in fostering and adoption and opened the field so that those now accepted are more representative of the families found in the community (ABSWAP, 1981).

Trapped by institutionalised racism, a conviction about the superiority of their own culture, ignorance about other people's culture, personal anxieties about risk-taking in complex situations which become open to public scrutiny if they are mishandled, and powerlessness in changing policy and practice, white social workers working on an individual-istic basis have become immobilised by their practice and cannot easily perceive and confront the negative features identified in it by black social workers in places like Lambeth. Their entrapment through these aspects of their practice ensures that white social workers minimise the risks they take by playing a cautious role or going by the book instead of either using their discretion or challenging the system. Thus they place black children in white families as their safest option. But exercising such choices pathologises black people and limits their right to self-determination.

White social workers should beware of promoting black people's right to self-determination in the absence of support from other black individuals and organisations in clarifying their objectives, and without the resources necess-ary for its realisation, for their intervention may be counter-productive. For example, placing a black child in a white family because the child and the parents wish it, without exploring the reasons behind their request is not encourag-ing client self-determination. Many black people have inter-nalised racist values pathologising black families (Lorde, 1984) and may be colluding with the white social worker's own racism. Equally, white social workers who pounce on black families to care for 'difficult to place black children', leaving the family unsupported in doing so, are not provid-ing an anti-racist service. They are being racist in so far as their actions depict an uncaring attitude suggesting second rate families are appropriate for second rate people. And they are being racist in expecting a black family to do the work they require without exploring its needs for additional resourcing and support.

White social workers' handling of the Jasmine Beckford family reveals a further salient point. That it was white social workers in a predominantly white department working with a black child and her black family is seldom mentioned, even in Blom-Cooper's report, *A Child in Trust*. Yet 'race' is a crucial aspect of the dynamics in the case, not only because racism adversely affects black people, but also because white people are afraid to confront the issue. They are scared stiff that if they do so, they will be accused of being racist (Comer, 1972; Banks, 1971). Knowing oneself – one's fears, aspirations and values – and using this knowledge in the casework relationship is central to traditional concepts of good social work practice (Compton and Galaway, 1975, p.143). If white social workers do not address racism directly, they are not coming to terms with their fears, thereby actively blocking interaction between them and black people. When racism is not considered relevant when it undoubtedly is, detrimental practice is initiated. Black people may pay with their lives for not getting the services they require. Or, as Banks (1971, p.137) warns: 'In the effort to help the black man [*sic*] . . . the issue of black and white becomes significant. Indeed, if this issue is not considered, much of the new effort to help the black man may go astray.'

Meanwhile, white social workers and their social services departments carry on oblivious to it all. The department and the white social worker have both failed the black client. The department has also failed white social workers. For their difficulty in confronting racism, including their own, is not being addressed. If white social workers can acknowledge racism as an issue and as a problem for them, it is easier for them to refer black clients to other black people or organisations who can provide the appropriate services, and get the support they need in overcoming their racism and anxieties about it.

In other situations, race may be acknowledged slightly, but as a problem which cannot be tackled. Sometimes, lack of resources is used as a reason for not doing so, e.g. not providing Sikh elders with Sikh home helps because the

Department does not employ any and additional home helps are unavailable as services are being cut back. In other instances, statutory agencies transfer their obligation to provide facilities for all client groups to the voluntary sector. Voluntary organisations run primarily by white people are often used by social services departments to avoid establishing anti-racist services themselves. Social services departments have at times formed poorly-funded voluntary agencies to provide cheap 'band-aid' services for black people. By evading their responsibilities, management in statutory agencies colludes with and perpetuates racist social work policies and practices. In so far as voluntary organisations try to plug gaps in statutory provisions, they are colluding with institutional racism, enabling social services departments to avoid developing adequate services for black people. Moreover, because voluntary bodies are usually badly equipped in anti-racist terms, black clients continue to receive inappropriate services. The following case, presented to me as an example of 'successful intervention in a black family', makes this point and demonstrates the process whereby black families are clientised.

A health visitor referred Indejit, a Sikh woman who spoke Punjabi but virtually no English, to the local social services district team because she was 'suffering from post-natal depression after giving birth to a girl-child'. As there were no Punjabi-speaking black social workers in the team which had few referrals involving black people, a white English-speaking social worker went to do a home visit. She was welcomed into the home by Indejit and her eldest daughter, aged 9, whom the white social worker used as a translator. Following the visit, the white social worker decided that the social services department had nothing to offer: 'Indejit seemed alright'. She was merely experiencing the 'normal let-down in Asian families after giving birth to four (successive) daughters'. But the white social worker thought 'Indejit was lonely', so she asked a voluntary agency to see her in a 'befriending way and help her learn English'. The voluntary agency in question operated on a shoe-string budget including some funding from social services which had initiated its formation several years earlier. It did not have any black Punjabi-speaking workers either. But it wanted to demonstrate its lack of prejudices by making itself available to the black community, so they sent along their best worker, Sue – a sensitive older white woman who 'would be a friend to Indejit and teach her English'. The white worker and Indejit 'got on well'. Indejit learnt some English and Sue got invited to many of the family's festive occasions. Although Sue noticed Indejit looking neither well nor happy, she did not broach the subject of Indejit's 'depression'. She felt she need not worry about it because Indejit had been seeing her 'GP who had put her on tranquillisers'. Yet when Sue left the agency and another worker, Ros, took her place, she discovered, quite by accident, that Indejit was being regularly physically abused by her husband. Yet she did nothing to ensure Indejit's safety. Ros claimed: 'There was nothing I could do. There's no women's refuge in the town, let alone an Asian women's one. And social services said there was nothing they could do since the children were safe.'

This case is obviously one in which collusion with institutionalised racism and sexism is occurring on a massive scale. Within the social services department, institutionalised racism flourishes because management has abrogated its responsibility with respect to black clients, e.g. providing Punjabi-speaking black workers who could have made a proper assessment of Indejit's needs. And no one else is taking up the issue of the lack of services appropriate to the needs of black people. The voluntary agency colludes with this institutionalised racism because it accepts responsibility for the case when it is not equipped to do so. The white social worker personally colluded with institutional racism by a) making an assessment visit knowing she was unable to communicate with Indejit, and not taking steps to overcome this problem by demanding her department employ a Punjabi-speaking black social worker; b) making judgments on the nature of the problem without sufficient evidence to back these; c) using racist stereotypes to justify further inaction; and d) keeping quiet about the department's general failure to address the needs of black people. The white voluntary workers colluded with the racism displayed in the handling of the case by accepting the white social worker's assessment of the problem to be addressed, and not responding to the issue of domestic violence.

Indejit needed someone she could speak to directly and who would be able to understand her specific situation. In terms of making an adequate response to her possible, knowing that it did not have the requisite skilled personnel to hand, the social services department should have tried to get hold of a Punjabi-speaking Sikh social worker. In the short-term, Britain is not so vast a country that social services departments which have the excuse that 'there are very few black families' living in their areas and therefore it is 'uneconomic to employ black workers' are unable to develop links with other authorities which recruit black staff. Regional links between several authorities with extra payments to black workers available for working in different parts of the region could be set in motion easily and quickly by management. Authorities which are located in areas where communities of black people live should employ sufficient black staff to provide the services these communities need. In the long term, black social workers should be found in all parts of Britain, irrespective of whether or not black communities are located within a social services department's boundaries. White anti-racist social workers, knowing their limitations, would press their department to acquire the resources they need to provide black people with appropriate services and develop links with relevant black organisations.

Moreover, Indejit's case illustrates how employing institutions ride on white workers' sympathies and 'desire to offer something' to those they know would otherwise get no service, despite their needs. Employers are exploiting white social workers' humanity by forcing them to provide an inadequate and inappropriate service, thereby making them poor practitioners and less human in the process. Meanwhile, they are saving money. Providing poorly-equipped workers to do a task they cannot handle has become one way in which employers use racism to ration their resources and give black clients the message that their needs are no great concern of theirs.

Both the white social worker and the white voluntary workers are reinforcing institutionalised sexism, i.e. not making available specific provisions to meet women's needs as women, by not considering Indejit's personal needs important enough for intervention in their own right. Instead, they relate to her as a mother who had to be kept 'coping' with her family responsibilities, responding only to those aspects of her situation they deemed potentially disruptive of her ability to look after her children.

White social workers should also appreciate the power structures and dynamics within black families and the alterations engendered in these by racism. Their failure to do so is evident in the inappropriate involvement of black children to plug gaps left by inadequate service provisions, e.g. using black children as interpreters. The use of children at all as interpreters is questionable (Ahmed, 1978). Such exploitation of black children is racist because it facilitates the continuation of inadequate services for black people. When it happens, the black child becomes an integral part of the interaction between black people and powerful white agencies and bureaucracies. The black child's knowledge of English becomes a tool for undermining parental authority. Additionally, the child might not understand either the nature of the problem under discussion or the subtleties of the language being used.

Inappropriate interpreters and translators have been used for several decades to cut costs because they are cheaper to employ than qualified black social workers. Translation is a highly skilled task if done properly. Using makeshift methods relying on whoever is available for this delicate work is a racist crisis response to the lack of appropriate services. It trivialises and devalues this activity. The development of a comprehensive translation service is necessary in establishing anti-racist social work. White social workers can make better use of their time and energies fighting racism by refusing to exploit black children for translation purposes and demand appropriate facilities instead. Translation services should be publicly funded and provide interpreters matched to clients' ethnic grouping, language, religion, class and gender. The provision of interpreters is not an alternative to employing black social workers. Establishing such a service provides a venue through which white social workers can contribute towards ensuring black people have equal access to mainstream facilities rather than ghettoised ones.

The convergence of white sexism and racism in social work practice

Institutionalised sexism – the casting of women in the role of carer; the definition of men as breadwinners and 'head' of the family; and the placing of children in a dependent status – combines with white people's racism to subordinate black family forms to the white middle-class heterosexual nuclear one. Institutionalised sexism also fuses with racism to ensure that black women's specific needs are seen as secondary to their responsibilities to their families. White social workers' stereotypes of black women make them particularly prone to integrating sexism with racism when intervening in the lives of black women and girls. Here, too, racist assumptions that white ways are the best ways underpin white social workers' handling of black women. White people use white cultural supremacy when judging Asian 'arranged' marriages inferior to Western 'romantic' marriages. This enables them to redefine 'arranged marriages' as 'marriages of convenience', i.e. phoney marriages. By not facilitating the acceptance of arranged marriages as the expression of loving relationships endorsed by a larger collectivity than the two individuals entering the marriage contract, the idea that arranged marriages are phoney marriages legitimates their being treated as inconsequential by white people and their institutions. This in turn allows white people to start treating black families as if there were no marriage contract and no family to preserve. Conceptualising black families in this fashion makes it easier for white people to ignore the extended ties and relationships existing among them. This includes deprecating black families for preferring boy children, even though white families express similar preferences (Oakley, 1972) and ignoring the ties which black fathers have with their children (*Ebony*, 1986).

Acting as if women in the West have achieved liberation, white social workers end up 'putting down' other people's achievements. In saying this, I am not suggesting that sexism should be condoned in any culture. But when white social workers work with black women and black girls wishing to escape the bounds of their particular form of sexism, they should not assume that black women demanding action in their specific situation are rejecting their culture and opting for an Anglo-Saxon life-style. Nor should they convey the impression that white women are free from gender oppression and can tell others what to do. It is not up to white men or women to tell black men and women how to run their lives (Lorde, 1984; Amos and Parmar, 1984; Carby, 1982). Sexism is already an issue black feminists are pursuing in their communities as a matter for them to resolve (Lorde, 1984; Carby, 1982). Meanwhile, black feminists have exposed the racism underpinning white feminists' presentation and understanding of gender oppression within black communities (Amos and Parmar, 1984; Parmar, 1982; Carby, 1982; Bryan, 1985). White anti-racist social workers are required to take seriously the issue of gender oppression in their own communities (Marchant and Wearing, 1986; Brook and Davis, 1985; Dominelli, 1984; Statham, 1978). Thus, uncovering racist practices in social work has also unearthed the sexism generally prevalent in social work practice and raised the issue of improving the position of white women as well.

Ideally, until white social workers become anti-racist and anti-sexist, they should not intervene in the lives of black women. But, if white social workers find themselves supporting black women who have taken decisions to break from their community, they should explore with them the impact white racism will have on their decision, particularly the isolation, sexual harassment, racial harassment and lack of resources they will encounter. Being aware of the disruption such action causes black women's relationships with their families and communities, white social workers' task is to facilitate their contacting other black women and black support groups sharing their particular views or needs. Although they may encounter community opposition, black women's support networks and resources can provide the space within which black women can decide what they want to do with their lives and receive support in maintaining their decision. White social workers facilitating such contacts should be aware of their existence.

a.   *The expression of white sexism in a case involving a black woman*

Such knowledge is important if white social workers are helping black women escape difficult domestic situations, e.g. black women wishing to leave battering husbands. Simply encouraging black women to leave and take their chances in white society would constitute racist practice. White social workers must discuss with black women the racist white society into which they will enter alone once they leave the protection of their community and its familiar surroundings and support networks unless steps are taken to counteract this. The following account gives an indication of the difficulties black women encounter when they are 'helped' by well-meaning white social workers.

> A young, British-born Muslim woman, Fatima, asked a white social worker to help her leave her arranged marriage because her husband refused to allow her to go to college and pursue a career. Fatima insisted on total secrecy for fear that either her husband or her relatives would find out and prevent her from leaving – with force if necessary. The white social worker agreed because 'Here was a woman crying to be free of an arranged marriage.' However, he was only able to organise accommodation for Fatima in a town far away, where she knew no one. Her first encounter with the DHSS – claiming supplementary benefit – was a nightmare, riddled with racial harassment and racist and sexist innuendo. Whilst queuing, she was told, 'Go back to your husband and let him keep you. We don't want you . . . scrounging on the state.' The poor woman was devastated by the ordeal. She felt lonely and homesick and missed contact with her mother.

This is an example of white naivety reinforcing and exacerbating the Muslim woman's experience of both racism and sexism. The sexism the white social worker has tried to avoid has been intensified through his racism.

The tasks for white social workers working with black women are becoming sufficiently aware of black women's networks and resources for referring black women to those sharing their views or undergoing similar experiences; and joining alliances endorsing black women's demands for adequate funding for their support groups and networks. For anti-racist relationships to develop, both the funds and the campaign for which the alliance has been created should be controlled by black women. Guru (1987) presents a powerful case for more welfare resources being made available to Asian women for funding refuges, workers and activities challenging oppression. White social workers can endorse these and similar demands and put pressure on their authorities to release funds without strings attached. They can also campaign against the law depriving voluntary organisations of their charitable status if they promote issues challenging institutionalised racism because the state considers such activities 'political' (Guru, 1987). White social workers can expose the political nature of the law which allows racism to persist through this definition of the matter. The intervention of white social workers depicted here demonstrates how acting on racism brings community action and campaigning techniques into social work, thereby combining personal with structural change.

b. *The expression of white sexism in a case involving child abuse*

White social workers' views of the black family as pathological can often lock black families into long-term intervention disadvantaging them. The following case study involving child abuse highlights the variety of ways in which sexism combines with racism. It is suitable for clarifying issues and identifying:

a. sources of cultural racism, institutionalised racism, and personal racism, including the links between them;
b. elements of bad practice including sexism and racism.

A white health visitor referred the Patel family to the social services department shortly after the birth of twins – a boy and a girl, because she considered the care of the girl twin inadequate. She thought the girl child was being rejected and neglected by her mother because the family 'had wanted more sons'. The Patels had two other children, a boy aged 3 and a girl aged 2. A white social worker who did not speak Gujerati, the language the family used in communicating with each other, visited them regularly to:

    a. advise the mother generally on caring for her babies; and
    b. check and discuss the mother's relationship with the girl twin.

Her involvement with the family continued for one year, when Mrs Patel became pregnant again. When she was due to give birth, the twins were received into care. The male twin was returned home promptly following the birth of the third son, but the girl twin remained in care for a year whilst white social workers made intensive visits to the Patels to encourage the mother to prepare herself for her daughter's return. Meanwhile, little contact occurred between mother and daughter, for she was being fostered by a white family some distance away. When the girl twin was returned home, the white social worker provided a day nursery place for her, a home help for her mother, some financial assistance for her unemployed father, accommodation advice for rehousing the family whose two-bedroomed terrace was too small, and a white voluntary worker to 'befriend Mrs Patel' by providing language tuition. The 'support of the mother' lasted four years. During this time, the mother's relationship with the girl twin improved, and the case was closed. Three years later, the case was reopened on suspicion that the girl twin was being physically abused. She displayed 'problem behaviour' at home and school. The family requested she be taken into care. The social work intervention this time consisted of:

    a. intensive home visits;
    b. counselling and advice for Mr and Mrs Patel regarding the 'care and control' of their girl twin; and
    c. liaison between the school and the parents.

This intervention continued for two years and the situation improved. The case was then closed.

White social workers saw the Patels two years later when writing reports for the Juvenile Court for the girl twin and her youngest brother. Both had been truanting. This time their intervention focused on:

a. regular home visits;
b. advising and counselling Mrs Patel; and
c. helping the girl twin organise her leisure time more effectively.

The girl twin was received into care for three weeks to provide the family with space for re-evaluating their views of her. The parents subsequently discharged her from care. The case was closed anew.

This was followed by intermittent involvement at the family's request for advice regarding care and control of the girl twin whose behaviour continued to deteriorate. Meanwhile, the police became concerned about her behaviour, as did the school. She was subsequently moved to a special school with smaller classes offering firm control over its pupils. The girl's behaviour improved slightly. A short time later, the Juvenile Court requested further reports, for the girl was being charged with theft and criminal damage. After the report was completed, further social work intervention seemed unnecessary. So the case was closed.

This case study is riddled with instances of personal, institutional and cultural racism interconnecting with each other, sexism, and bad practice. Illustrating the social working of black families, it provides a horrific example of the processes involved in their clientisation. Although discussion on it can cover a number of aspects, I will focus on only a few. Cultural racism is evident in the defining of black families' child-rearing practices as inferior to white ones, particularly in the handling of girl children. This is particularly evident in the instruction of the mother in 'approved', i.e. white, child care practices. Cultural racism is also expressed in the white social worker's request for a white voluntary worker to 'befriend' the mother and teach her English. The white health visitor's individual racism is conveyed through her assumption that black families treat boy children better because they are preferred to girls. Yet, as she did not speak Gujerati, it is hard to visualise how she acquired the evidence to reach this conclusion. Institutionalised racism is depicted by the social services department's failure to provide a black Gujerati-speaking worker who could have properly assessed the problem(s) that required addressing instead of immediately tackling the 'presenting' one. Also, the unspecific nature of the department's responses suggest its workers do not take seriously the needs of black clients.

Racism in these varied forms was integrated into the work to produce a catalogue of bad practice spanning thirteen years. It included: not having an adequate system for evaluating, assessing and processing the referral; the failure of both health and social services departments to provide language facilities in the appropriate mother tongue; not providing the family with a black worker to communicate effectively with them; concentrating intervention on the girl child and her mother, ignoring the needs of the boy children and the father's involvement in their upbringing; not facilitating contact between the girl twin and her parents when she was in care; emphasising the desirability of the family keeping their children well-behaved and under control rather than looking at their needs for growth and development; and limiting their resourcing of the family to advice and practical help in areas compatible with their analysis. Thus, for example, the father's employment prospects are not specifically addressed. Instead, constantly reinforcing labels of inadequate mothering, emphasising control, opening and closing the case without due regard for the actual needs of the individuals concerned, mark the poor practice here.

Good anti-racist practice would have ensured both the health service and social services had black employees who could have spoken directly to the family and addressed their actual needs. Had this occurred, they might have challenged the assertion that preferring boy children leads to the mistreatment of girls and discovered what the real problems were. The case before us would then have been very different.

White social work intervention with black youth

Youth in general and black youth in particular currently has few opportunities for contributing to society in significant ways and acquiring a sense of belonging to it. Society's major concern with youth has been to control the rebellious elements threatening its fragile stability (Dominelli, 1983). This task has become increasingly difficult as the 'Crisis of policing [the] working class city has become a crisis of legitimacy for the bourgeois public realm as a whole' (Cohen, 1979, p.136). Black youth, carrying white society's stigma for causing inner city malaise, are considered its greatest threat (CCCS, 1982). Everything about them – their lifestyles, relationships with one another and with authority – is defined as problematic by white people. White social workers working in inner city areas incorporate these definitions of 'the problem' into their work, thereby pathologising the young black population.

Because white people pathologise blacks by treating them rather than racism as the problem, black people's activities resisting racism receive similar treatment. Black males are penalised for having 'deviant' life-styles when they participate in action rejecting racism and positing positive self-identification as black men, e.g. Rastafarianism. White social workers pathologise such behaviour to justify their racist stereotypes and institutionalise young black men within the welfare and 'law and order' apparatuses.

White people's perceptions of black youths are largely influenced and defined by their contacts with the 'law and order apparatus' and the moral panics arising out of their alleged relationship with crime (Hall, 1978). Central to these is their expectation that black youth will be effectively contained and controlled by their own communities. As Rex puts it in respect of one group: 'Asian youth . . . have ready to hand a highly effective communal economic, social and political system to help them cope with the exigencies of life in an alien land (Rex, 1982, p.62). Points at which black youth either individually or collectively reject white demands for such conformity trigger white responses aimed at reasserting both external control initiated by the white community, especially its police force, and internal control imposed by 'the black community' through family ties and allegiance to its 'leaders'. The expectation that black youth be controlled by other black people becomes another avenue through which black communities are considered inadequate and pathologised by white people when black youth 'get out of control'. Black youth's rebellion over the police's handling of social relations on the Broadwater Estate illustrates this. The failure of the black community and its leadership to discipline its youth and keep its activities confined to those acceptable to white authority, resulted in the whole estate being stigmatised, labelled inadequate and subjected to intensive policing and external control (Loney, 1986).

The relationship between black youths and the police is highly problematic because the police, in upholding a racist society, amplify black youths' 'deviance' and exacerbate the difficulties they endure when they refuse to comply with 'soft' forms of social control (Moore, 1975). The police claim 'West Indian boys get into trouble because they are out of control'; Asian lads do so because of problems 'arising from violence and the enforcement of discipline or fighting for the control of institutions' (Rex, 1982, p.61). Reinforcing notions of being out of control in blaming black youth for resisting institutionalised racism becomes the means whereby the forces of 'law and order' instigate tighter surveillance of black youths and their communities and contain their activities. This adds a further twist in the mechanisms through which black youths and black communities are pathologised and socially controlled. The measures proposed in the Scarman Report fail to tackle institutionalised racism of this form and place undue emphasis on pathologising racist individuals within the police force.

In social work, this expectation of internal community control, docility and 'looking after one's own' means that activities white social workers tolerate in white clients become alarming in black families, e.g. juvenile crime, adolescent struggles for individual autonomy. To allay their fears, white social workers encase black people in a web of stricter surveillance and control, rapidly clientising them as a host of welfare agencies descend upon them.

The idea that black youths are constantly out of control and liable to get into trouble accounts for white social workers' and probation officers' failure to ensure that the black youths referred to them for a variety of offenses receive equal treatment with white youths. Institutionalised racism in the procedures adopted in handling black youths' contacts with the law causes their civil liberties to be more easily disregarded than white youths' and leads to their being clientised at the heavy end of the sentencing tariff (Tipler, 1986). Hutchinson-Reis, describing his work as a social worker on the Broadwater Farm Estate, depicts the difficulties his team had in protecting the rights of young black people charged with offences following the 'uprising' there. He makes it clear young blacks needed social work intervention aimed at securing justice from both the police and courts. As he says: 'Juveniles were often intimidated by the thought of murder or affray charges being brought against them if they did not co-operate with the police investigation' (Hutchinson-Reis, 1986, p.76). Both black and white social workers following casework models of intervention have been unable to stop the blatant disregard of black youths' rights because they were being 'severely obstructed' and 'denied the opportunity to perform that function' (Hutchinson-Reis, 1986, p.76). Moreover, black social workers involved in these attempts, have found institutional restraints adversely affect them by compromising and negating their racial and political integrity (Hutchinson-Reis, 1986, p.79). These processes have compelled social workers on the Broadwater Estate to work collectively to empower themselves and deliver a more appropriate service to clients. By challenging individualistic casework approaches to their work these dynamics were initially modified and subsequently ruptured. Hutchinson-Reis calls their new techniques 'community social work'. His description of these reveals his team's efforts were based on community action principles transcending one-to-one methods of responding to individual clients' needs. Using new forms of organising:

'social workers with allocated cases of arrested juveniles began to meet weekly to share information, issues and discuss arrangements for working with the number of juveniles being arrested, detained, charged and remanded into care and needing placements' (Hutchinson-Reis, 1986, p.77). Collective action amongst social workers, regardless of whether they are black or white, is indispensable in tackling institutionalised racism and the constraints and controls to which workers are personally subject as part of their job.

White social workers' training and allegiance to their professional work ethics makes them particularly prone to rejecting collective working relations and misconstruing the significance of collectivities within the black community. The collective support of black families and communities is particularly important in providing black individuals with the psychological and material resources necessary for surviving in a racist world. The protection black collectivities offer black individuals is a significant force tying individuals and communities together in sets of mutual obligations towards one another (Lorde, 1984). Not grasping their centrality, white social workers pathologise black individuals' responsibilities towards their collectives and the support they derive from them. Within this framework, they label actions and behaviour affirming solidarity and collectivism amongst black people 'undesirable', those undermining them are confirmed as 'desirable'. Thus white social workers consider allegiance to black life-styles pathological.

Such dynamics become especially relevant in white social workers' intervention in cases defined as 'problems with arranged marriages', or 'generational conflicts'. White social workers responding to the impact of black collectives by pathologising them should not work with black people. They are likely to intervene inappropriately and cause further hardship to them. Relating this to black youth, white social workers assume that any questioning of their collective framework is a vilification of it. White social workers should not perceive conflict between black children and their parents as automatically implying either a rejection of their cultural values or a preference for British ones (Ahmed,

1978). These are areas to be explored and the wishes of the black client established openly, rather than interpreting whatever they say in terms that white social workers want to hear. Black youth establishing their own parameters in life are just as likely to rebel against parental authority during adolescence as white youth.

Black social workers have provided alternative models for black youths and have organised forms of intervention celebrating their achievements. These enable black youths to develop their individual potential and build their own specific sense of self-identity. White social workers should refer black youths to such provisions, e.g. the Handsworth Alternative Scheme (Rhamdanie, 1978).

White social work intervention with older black people

Older people currently constitute a small proportion of the black population (Bhalla, 1981; Holland 1986). But they have been virtually neglected by statutory bodies and have seldom found provisions addressing their specific needs (Farrah, 1986; Holland, 1986). Part of the reason for their exclusion has been social services departments' traditional concern with children, rather than older people. Choosing to spend their limited resources on statutory obligations, social services departments have colluded with the ageist nature of British society as well as its racism. Another reason has been the young age of the black population in this country (Holland, 1986). However none of these reasons justifies the lack of provisions where it is needed. Myths about the support of the extended family in caring for its older members have also been used by white social workers and their institutions to deny the need for making appropriate provisions available. This way of approaching the situation ignores the racist immigration laws which have engendered divisions in the extended family spreading it across several continents. Also resettlement patterns separating extended family members entering Britain have hindered the re-creation of extended family networks, e.g. the dispersal of Ugandan Asian refugees. Moreover, the lack of material resources, especially in income and housing (Smith, 1976; Brown, 1984), does not facilitate the development of networks of this type. Consequently, substantial numbers of black elders have no family members in Britain. Bhalla (1981, p.33) has found that 26 per cent of Asians and 9 per cent of Afro-Caribbean elders are in this position.

Unequal access to incomes is a particular problem for elders who have entered Britain as sponsored dependents for they are not entitled to income support or supplementary benefit. This remains the case even in instances in which their sponsors, who may have been able to provide for them at the time of entry, can no longer do so, because of unemployment, sickness, or old age themselves. The implications of this are quite disturbing, given disparities in state support for different ethnic groups. For example, Bhalla (1981, p.17) has revealed that whilst 94 per cent of European and 83 per cent of Afro-Caribbean elders receive state pensions, only 46 per cent of Asian ones do. Moreover, 32 per cent of these do not get full pensions. Age Concern in Lewisham discovered that one quarter of black elders were not receiving full pension entitlements. Black people's low earnings levels mean they are also denied the possibility of saving, purchasing private pension plans, or acquiring sufficient contributions to increase their pension levels through state-inspired earnings-related schemes.

Most local authorities do not have an accurate description of the numbers of elders from black communities living within their borders, let alone an analysis of their needs (Farrah, 1986; Holland, 1986). Others, e.g. Coventry, have undertaken surveys highlighting ethnic elders and their needs, with limited practical outcomes (Holland, 1986). Local authorities' failure to take seriously their responsibilities towards older black people is reflected in their inadequate service provisions. These include: a) few facilities available specifically for them; b) not informing them of the limited service provided; c) the low take-up of services which are on offer; d) offering inappropriate services; and e) expecting older black people to be assimilated into the white British way of life.

The failure of local authorities to inform black people of the limited services specifically provided for them means that few black people are aware of what is available, and therefore are not likely to demand these provisions. The Bhalla study reveals that whilst 64 per cent of Asian elders are not aware of the welfare provisions available to them, only 2 per cent of white elders share their fate. Bhalla (1981, p.29) also indicates that 19 per cent of European elders have home-helps, but only 9 per cent of Afro-Caribbean and no Asian elders do so. Many Asian elders cannot use Meals-On-Wheels because they do not cater for their specific dietary requirements. Yet, Holland's work (1986, p.28) suggests that 15 per cent of Asian elders want vegetarian Meals-On-Wheels, and 11 per cent would like Asian home helps. The view that older black people are expected to adopt the white British life-style is reflected in the opinions expressed by practitioners. These were articulated as follows by a white care assistant when I interviewed her: 'We cannot provide for ethnic minorities here. It wouldn't be fair to the others. No, I treat them all the same. It's the only way.'

If white social workers could actively seek and respond to consumers' assessments of their services, improvements could be fostered. For example, matching workers, including care assistants and home-helps, with the elders into whose lives they enter could be pressed as a matter of priority. The attitude of indifferent neglect regarding the use of English as the language of communication could be challenged. Leaflets could be translated into other ethnic languages. Bhalla's (1981, p.14) study found that 88 per cent of older people from the Indian sub-continent do not speak English. The Holland (1986, p.9) research reveals only 11 per cent of the ethnic elders interviewed speak English. Yet there is not even an interpreting service available for them. Local authorities could provide ethnic elders with translation facilities. Black workers could be employed to work specifically with them.

It is inappropriate for social services departments to pretend that developing the services needed by black elders is an 'immigrant problem that will go away'. Most black elders have settled permanently in Britain. Bhalla indicates that 85 per cent of the Asian and 67 per cent of the Afro-Caribbean elderly expect to stay permanently in Britain. However, the numbers may actually be much higher as only 8 per cent of the Asian group and 6 per cent of the Afro-Caribbean group have actively made plans to return to their country of origin (Bhalla, 1981, p.33). This, combined with the relative youthfulness of black elders, suggests their needs will become more pressing in the future. Thus social services departments should begin planning now so that services can be available when needed.

Black self-help groups have tried to compensate for the widespread dereliction of duty perpetrated by statutory agencies against black elders by providing services of their own (Asian's Sheltered Residential Accommodation Association, 1981; Holland, 1986), e.g. day centres, sheltered accommodation. These provisions are locally based so that independence, dignity, and links between black communities and their elders can be maintained, and their religious, shopping, and companionship needs met. Residential accommodation for black elders have wardens and workers who speak their mother tongues; the aids necessary for coping with the disabilities of old age; small units providing both private and communal facilities rather than large institutionalised accommodation; a mix of people to include both able-bodied people and those with disabilities (ASRA, 1981; Farrah, 1986). Consequently, the provisions black people make available challenge the ageism as well as the racism endemic in Britain.

Whilst this response by black self-help groups is essential in the short term to pick up on the pressing needs of individuals enduring hardship, this does not resolve the matter. For statutory institutions continue neglecting black elders' needs, thereby perpetuating their racist and discriminatory practices. Black youths are now questioning the diversion of black people's energies through self-help organisations. Claiming that black self-help projects have negligible impact on institutionalised racism, they argue these organisations have little clout in transforming broader social relations (Gilroy, 1987). Moreover, these self-help initiatives do not provide the full range of services that are required because they are seriously under-resourced. Black people are also concerned that their self-help projects have become measures through which the state keeps militant blacks occupied (Mullard, 1973). Black people's growing unease over the use of black self-help initiatives for avoiding public responsibility in making these provisions available is justified. An example of such evasion has recently occurred in Royal Leamington Spa. Following a detailed examination of the issue, the local Community Relations Council asked Warwick District Council to provide 'special sheltered housing units for Asians'. Their extended families could not do so. Suggesting this description of Asian elders 'special needs' was inaccurate, the Council's chief executive officer responded that a further study was necessary to assess the situation. But, a local councillor proclaimed, 'I am fundamentally opposed to any form of segregation' (*Coventry Evening Telegraph*, 1987). Besides revealing that white authorities prefer white scientific analyses to black ones, this suggests special provisions are not segregation if provided by the Asian community through its own resources.

Countering white social workers' racism

This chapter reveals the importance of white social workers questioning the appropriateness of their current intervention in black families. The accounts provided reveal that the imposition of racist value judgments on black families and their life-styles has been detrimental to their welfare and provides good reason for concluding white social workers should not work with black families until they have demonstrated their ability to practice anti-racist social work. The white social workers in the examples considered above require help in overcoming their racism. Doing so entails exposing the anglocentric nature of their thinking, and providing materials for them to learn about black people and their life-styles. It also requires addressing white society's racism. Racism cannot be countered simply by employing black social workers charged with developing 'services for their communities' within mainstream agencies. For unless social services departments take active steps to prevent it, they may end up 'dumping' their responsibility for eliminating racism on black employees (Rooney, 1980). Using black workers to work primarily with black clients can be no more than a temporary measure if their ghettoisation is to be avoided. Whilst black social workers provide positive models for black youths, and enhance black people's sense of confidence and esteem over their status in white society, racism would be reinforced if they were held responsible for all or most of the work involving ethnic minority groups. The ensuing segregation would deny black social workers scope to practice their skills outside their own ethnic grouping and acquire competence in fields other than those involving black ethnicity. Furthermore, in a racist society black people could perceive white powerholders' adherence to such allocation procedures as discriminatory, conveying the impression that black social workers are second-rate employees capable of working only with second-rate, i.e. black, clients (Mizio, 1972; Kadushin, 1972). Ghettoising black social workers allows white social workers to escape confronting their own racism. They could comfort themselves with the knowledge that now black people had black social workers, they would be getting the services they needed, ending their concern with racism. Operating in these terms challenges neither institutional racism, nor the individual racism of white clients.

White social workers should work in anti-racist ways so that black social workers can have real choices about the areas in which they would like to work, and clients have access to the services they need. Thus, alongside the employment of black workers, agency policy and practice must encompass the retraining of all white staff members in anti-racist directions. Eliminating racism at the individual level is a complicated task requiring long-term work with white people in both one-to-one and group settings. White individuals' progress on this can be monitored, and only when they have demonstrated their commitment to working in anti-racist ways, should they be employed in social work. Those indicating a willingness to learn how to work with ethnic groups other than their own need to work as apprentices under black workers who can assess and monitor their work from a black perspective.

The project of white social workers becoming anti-racists could be begun by employers giving them paid leave to undertake anti-racism awareness training and plan a personalised programme for change. Such a proposal could be implemented more successfully if participants were not stigmatised as 'racists' when *all white people are involved in perpetuating racism in some form*. Labelling of this nature could be avoided if anti-racism awareness training were incorporated into office routines and every white member of the team expected to take part in it. This could be complemented through the introduction of the Anti-Racist Apprenticeship Model of Social Work along the lines described in Chapter 2.

White social workers committed to developing anti-racist social work practice and ultimately intending to work with black families need special training to make them:

a. culturally aware from an anti-racist perspective, that is, able to understand the significance of cultural factors without laying the responsibility for everything that goes wrong at culture's door;

b. overcome the use of value judgments presupposing the superiority of white British culture and norms;

c. conscious of the impact of institutionalised racism on their work and commit themselves to fighting it;

d. explore the impact of white power and privileges in their relationships with black people;

e. draw connections between racism and the social control elements of social work; and

f. draw connections between eliminating racism and getting rid of other forms of oppression.

In addition, it is not enough for white social workers developing anti-racist practice to rely on their personal commitment to see them through to successful anti-racist intervention in a black family. White social workers wishing to develop anti-racist social work practice have no option but to initiate the organisational process of changing the perceptions, commitments and behaviour of colleagues, managers, employers and clients in this direction. Employers would have to commit themselves to introducing anti-racist policies and practices in their agency, thus providing the climate and back up support necessary for promoting racial equality and anti-racist social work. Getting this proposal incorporated into office policy and practice may entail a long and difficult struggle.

White clients should be encouraged through anti-racist policies and practice, to choose black social workers. Simply offering clients a choice about the ethnic origins of the worker to whom they relate, is not an appropriate way of embarking on this process. It merely increases the hurtfulness directed at black social workers. Striking a balance between agency policy when it is publicly committed to fighting racism, and the professed inclinations of individual workers and clients may be tricky in instances in which racism remains endemic. Initially, priority should be given to raising consciousness about racism as an issue, subsequently introducing procedures for eliminating racist practices. To make offering black social workers to white clients a positive experience for black workers, agencies would first have to challenge white clients' racist stereotypes about which social workers are appropriate for them. Clients would need anti-racism awareness training and support in exploring their reactions.

Black clients who have internalised white racism may also reject black social workers. They too need support. Anti-racist policies and practices can foster the circumstances in which both black and white clients would be able to relate to black social workers. White social workers faced with black clients preferring white social workers should explore the reasons for their 'choice' with them and ascertain whether it stems from internalised racism. If this is the case, they should be referred to black social workers capable of working with them on this issue. Anti-racist policies and practices can foster circumstances in which both black and white clients can relate to black social workers.

Agencies should provide black workers with support in dealing with rejection from white clients, white colleagues, or other black people. Having a well-known and adhered to equal opportunities policy containing penalties such as fines for overt racist statements and comments from workers, and a refusal to provide clients with services if they harass black workers or clients, goes some way towards providing this. White workers who practice racial harassment should be disciplined and, if necessary, dismissed as incompetent for doing their job. To implement this effectively and justly, employing authorities must develop well publicised and understood grievance procedures covering racial harassment. These should secure justice for black people and initially allow white people the opportunity of altering their behaviour in accordance with anti-racist norms. There is also a strong case for white social workers to work alongside black groups challenging racism within professionalism by identifying potential resources, organisational norms and decision-making processes which these groups can tap into. In reversing the power relationships between them, white social workers would become anti-racist community advocates working alongside black people in a common cause. Equalising power differentials between them and black people would free white social workers to develop new ways of responding to black service users.

Because challenging racism exposes bad practices all round, the development of anti-racist social work practice enlarges the spectrum of choice available to both black and white people. Thus a strategy for tackling racism must be multi-faceted. From an anti-racist perspective, having one's welfare assured is a fundamental human right. All individuals are entitled to the welfare services they need – as of right, regardless of period of stay in this country, conditions of admission for residence, skin colour, religious affiliation, or linguistic capabilities.

5

Tackling Racism at the Organisational Level: Working on Agency Policies and Practices

Focusing on one's own practice and developing anti-racist struggles in relation to that is important, but gains brought about through individual effort will be limited unless changes are also wrought in agency policy and practices. Changes in agency policy and practices are necessary to provide the supportive foundation for consolidating, extending and developing further anti-racist social work practice undertaken by individual practitioners. Moreover, initiatives in this arena must be buttressed by anti-racist policies and practices in both the local and central state apparatuses. White social workers can begin engaging in the process of changing their own agency by a) ending their involvement in the conspiracy of silence which denies and ignores the prevalence of institutionalised and cultural racism in their organisation; b) organising in their workplace for the implementation of an equal opportunities policy; c) initiating and continuing the debate elaborating on the components of anti-racist social work practice; and d) establishing the machinery which will monitor progress on the realisation of anti-racist policies and practices in their agency. This will require white anti-racist social workers to develop alliances with other workers, management, politicians, trade unionists and others sharing their anti-racist goals. Such work contains risks which can affect the whole of their careers. Thus white social workers committed to anti-racist social work must prepare themselves for a rough ride in pursuing their goals as well as having the satisfaction of knowing that, through their efforts, justice will prevail and service delivery promoting welfare will be enhanced. White social workers should develop networks for their own survival in the crisis situations they will encounter as both personal, interpersonal and institutional resistance to their anti-racist activities come to the fore. Securing changes at the level of a particular agency requires additional resources as well as a more equitable use of existing ones. Finally, changes wrought at agency level must be guaranteed continuity and stability through more generalised support, including that of the local and central state. White social workers working collectively through their unions, professional associations, or organisations established specifically for this purpose, must put sustained collective pressure on the political apparatuses of local and central government to ensure they adopt and enforce anti-racist policies and practices through legislation, funding and establishing a climate fostering the further development of anti-racist social work. This chapter explores the ramifications of organisational change aimed at introducing and maintaining anti-racist social work.

Ending the conspiracy of silence about the presence of racism in social work

Keeping quiet about the many manifestations of racism in social work is a major way in which white people render the distressing experience of black people invisible. Silence also facilitates white people's collusion with this state of affairs, rendering them powerless in tackling it. For these reasons, white social workers must end the conspiracy of silence regarding the racism lying at the very heart of social work. In speaking out against it, white people become free to do something about eradicating racism and empowered in searching for ways of developing alliances based on equality with black people pitting their energies against it (Lorde, 1984).

When breaking this silence, white practitioners and educators will be compelled to:

1. verify and demonstrate the existence of racism in social work practice in its varied forms;
2. take a stand against these; and
3. work both individually and collectively in bringing about anti-racist policies and practices.

The implementation of these three strategies requires organisational change. Organisational change with respect to anti-racist social work covers two levels: a) employment policy and practice; and b) service delivery. In terms of employment policy and practice, black people must be employed in substantial numbers at all levels of an organisation under terms and conditions which do not undervalue their qualifications, expertise and career prospects, or dump the elimination of racism on their backs. In undertaking organisational change, the white anti-racist social worker will be challenging political priorities; legislation; professional ethics; management and its decisions in the allocation of both resources and power; policies; practice; colleagues; professional associations and trade unions; and clients.

Although you may feel powerless as a white individual with a commitment to introducing anti-racist social work in your agency, it is important that you do not feel discouraged from starting to raise the issue with others. Regardless of the level at which you find support for your views, the venture is worthy of your efforts. In many institutions, it has been the activities of individuals often carried out over a number of years, and at considerable personal cost to themselves, which have secured institutional commitment to equality of opportunity and anti-racist ways of working. Doing it on your own is the most difficult way of achieving these goals. It is much easier if you can become part of a group with similar commitments working on the matter.

Regardless of how you will be able to work within your organisation, the task will be difficult for a number of reasons. One is that white people committed to anti-racist ways of working find it problematic to translate their commitments to action when their own emotional or material interests are at stake. Another reason is that some people will feel it is not a problem in their particular setting, and will need convincing of the appropriateness of anti-racist action. Having an equal opportunities policy can foster anti-racist behaviour if it is linked to assessing people's performance on the job, thereby having a beneficial impact on your attempts to introduce change. While such a policy is unlikely to alter the views of people whose racism is based on dogma, it does promote a climate delegitimating the public expression of such opinions. To carry those people willing to engage personally in countering racism, such a policy must have with it the necessary resources and support networks. Difficulties are also encountered in introducing anti-racist social work because of the widespread belief among white people that working in anti-racist ways is optional. These individuals really do not understand the damage they inflict on black people's welfare through inaction or inappropriate action. As one social worker recently remarked at an anti-racist social work conference: 'I have a choice about whether or not I take up the fight against racism. And, if I decide to do so, it is up to me to decide the ways in which I do it.'

Besides highlighting the complexity of the problem and the difficulties white social workers have in working collectively against racism, this white woman, who saw herself as a sensitive social worker had a point. She does have a choice because as a white English person, racism is not directed at her. Neither she nor her close ones feel its barb of injustice. Being out of racism's direct impact makes her blind to the damage her view perpetrates on black people who suffer the effects of racism as she speaks. And it is they who continue to be wounded by racism because millions of other white people share her view. Moreover, her comments reveal her failure to connect the ravages racism wreaks on black people with the damage it is causing her. I am convinced that if the casualties of her involved, but blasé approach to racism could confront her in the shape of strong black people and herself visibly crippled by the words she spoke, this white woman would have been the first to recoil from her behaviour. And I am equally sure that its impact on her would have been profound enough to result in immediate behavioural change.

Moreover, once anti-racist change had been initiated in her behaviour, she would have felt compelled to seek institutional change so that others occupying her previous position would be moved to altering their ways. The difficulties white people have in making direct connections between their personal inaction and institutionalised oppression and its effect on individuals and groups make them tolerate morally reprehensible stances like that of having a 'choice' about tackling racism. Thus a considerable amount of work will have to be done by white anti-racist social workers with other white social workers who need convincing of the appropriateness of joining the campaign for anti-racist social work. Getting the agency to commit resources to retraining white people and sending them on anti-racism awareness training courses is an essential part of an institution's commitment to equal opportunities. These resources must not be diverted from those being required by black people to enter the institution in the first place or to receive the training they require while they are there. Thus implementing a policy of equal opportunities requires additional resourcing on both personal and institutional levels. While you are seeking alliances and organising with management, other workers, your trade unions and professional organisations to bring about an end to the conspiracy of silence and the declaration of an equal opportunities policy, you can continue your individual efforts in other aspects of your work, e.g. your relationships with black clients, raising the issue in team meetings, tackling racist comments wherever they occur.

It is important to counter racism regardless of the agency in which you work. Probation officers, social services departments, community work agencies, hospital settings and voluntary agencies each have specific forms of racism which must be overcome as well as forms which they hold in common with other organisations. Fighting racism requires agencies and individuals to acknowledge black people, their needs and their contributions to society; become familiar with work black people have already done in countering racism; challenge prevailing definitions of social work; and develop anti-racist policies and practice. At the forefront of the struggle against racism are a series of questions which white anti-racist social workers need to address. These are:

What needs doing?
By whom should it be done?
How is it to be done?
What targets need to be set?
What blockages will be encountered?
How can these be overcome?

Ending the conspiracy of silence also requires denouncing the invidious position in which organisations place black people allegedly employed as part of their strategy in combating racism. This means exposing the dumping of anti-racist work entirely on the shoulders of black staff; and exposing authorities which hinder the development of links between black staff and their communities for fear that black staff's accountability would be community-based rather than employer-based (see Rooney, 1980). Black people have become concerned that black professionals are being incorporated by the 'race relations' side of an organisation's work through their terms and conditions of employment. Others feel quite strongly that the whole 'race relations' apparatus has become another mechanism of social control for black people and their aspirations (Mullard, 1973; ALTARF, 1984).

The 'new' black professional middle class has been created by the 'race relations' apparatus which includes the CRE/CRC, local authorities, social services departments, and the educational system. Because of the racism endemic in these institutions, black workers occupy a contradictory position within them – as representatives of oppressed communities and as state employees forming part of the state apparatus (Mullard, 1973). The pressures on them, particularly those emanating from workload allocations, the decision-making processes and departmental priorities, incorporate them into its social control functions (Rooney, 1980; Gilroy, 1987).

Dealing with this contradiction becomes particularly difficult in a situation of scarce resources engendered through public expenditure cuts compelling black and white social workers to ration provisions across the largest number of clients. The need to implement such policies, whatever the justice of the cases being handled, often puts black social workers at odds with both their employer and their communities. Since race relations structures are multi-racial in the sense that they include both black and white members in their teams, it is important that their potential to incorporate and de-radicalise black people and their aspirations and the mechanisms whereby this is achieved are grasped. Otherwise subsequent anti-racist changes in these structures and in the reformulation of the 1976 Race Relations Act will be unable either to stem institutionalised racism, or to redefine black people's social status in them, or to reallocate black people's share of society's power and resources to them.

Moreover, the tendency of local authorities and the central state to employ people with attitudes coinciding with their own predisposes them into appointing small 'c' conservatives from within the black community (Rooney, 1980). The entry of such appointees into jobs with reasonable salaries and some form of long-term security distances them from the remainder of their community, particularly its working-class elements who have not been made party to white people's privileges. White social workers have commented on how black 'middle-class' people they have used in their work with black families have put black clients down. For example, one white social worker recalled how shocked she was when a 'middle-class' Brahmin woman called in to translate in the case of a Muslim woman from the Gujerat said of her client, 'She is really an ignorant peasant who doesn't understand very much.' There is an assumption amongst white social workers that black people should respect one another simply because they are black. And they believe that 'the black community's is homogeneous, when this is far from the case. Black people may have racism in common, but they are culturally, linguistically, socially, religiously, economically and politically diverse – just as Europeans are. White social workers should acknowledge the heterogeneity of black communities in their work, instead of perpetuating the racist stereotype that 'they are all the same'. In addition, they must not be lulled into mistakenly thinking racism does not affect black professionals because they are 'middle class'. The experience of 'middle-class' black professionals is not the same as 'middle-class' white professionals. The former's experience of racism will inevitably mediate their experience of class (Gilroy, 1987). Understanding these dynamics is a task white social workers have to undertake if they are to participate actively in ending the conspiracy of silence.

White anti-racist social workers can take measures aimed at convincing employing authorities to foster the creation and the maintenance of effective links between black professionals and their communities. This can be facilitated by employers actively encouraging their black workers to form black support groups and networks for themselves and other black people. Ending the conspiracy of silence in this respect requires white people to accept responsibility for drawing black professionals into power structures which isolate them from their communities, i.e. recognising that this distancing has been of our making. We can avoid placing black people in this position by not employing them as isolated individuals and providing them with the time, space and other resources necessary for developing black support groups and maintaining their community networks.

Opportunities of this nature are seldom made available to black social workers. Barney Rooney (1980), in a well-documented account of Liverpool's employment of black social workers as part of its attempt at increasing rapport between the social services department and the 'alienated' black community, mounts a scathing attack on an authority paying scant attention to the needs of its black staff. Rooney goes beyond this in her criticism and slates Liverpool on a number of counts. These are:

1. employing black social workers having little connection with the communities they are to serve other than the colour of their skin;
2. employing black social workers outside mainstream

career grades through the Urban Aid Programme and dispersing them throughout the city;
3. dumping the responsibility for handling all of the 'race' issues on their shoulders;
4. obliging them to work with black people within established priorities and methods of working, i.e. heavy workloads emphasising one-to-one work;
5. destroying black social workers' credibility with their communities.

Condemning Liverpool's actions as tokenist, defining the term as recruiting black 'people into an organisation to give the impression of change and then using them to consolidate resistance to change', Rooney (1980, p.48) argues that Liverpool devised its strategy of employing black workers to ensure that mainly black workers who would not challenge the organisation and its ways of working were appointed. Such a strategy, she maintains, enables the local authority to use black workers in controlling the community. Without close links with the community, because these workers did not come from Liverpool and lacking a shared experience of being at the receiving end of the department's services, Rooney maintains these black social workers were unable to develop forms of collective organisation which could effectively challenge the local authority's ways of working with black people, transform its definition of social work, develop appropriate forms of service delivery to black clients, and empower black people.

Rooney also declares that white people are hostile to black social workers because they fear their strengths, particularly their contacts with black communities and their ability to identify with black clients. Such skills are deemed 'unprofessional' by white social workers and white managers. Her comments have been backed in an interview I had with a district team manager who said: 'They [black social workers] demonstrate a capacity to get over-involved. We don't hold with social workers – any social worker, black or white – not being able to stand back and make a professional assessment of a situation.' But in Rooney's terms, the real problem for white employers is that black social workers with close links with their community will identify with black clients rather than their employers. For example, these differences are clearly manifest in the handling of confidentiality. The black social worker would extend the circle of confidentiality to include the client, the white organisation would not (Rooney, 1980). Additionally, white social workers and institutions subject black social workers to racial harassment – presuming them to be clients rather than workers on initial encounter; asking for their credentials, rather than taking their word for it. This description reveals black social workers experience anything other than equal opportunities when they are appointed social workers. Rectifying the situation requires taking positive steps to end the conspiracy of silence about such practices. Countering these also demands the implementation of an equal opportunities policy in its broadest sense.

Establishing an equal opportunities policy: setting the climate for anti-racist social work

Under the Race Relations Act 1976, all institutions providing services to the public are responsible for ensuring these are non-discriminatory, either directly or indirectly. Although government departments can plead immunity from its provisions, there is scope for using this legislation in getting your employer to formulate, adopt and implement an equal opportunities policy essential for creating a climate conducive to anti-racist social work. It is not, in itself, anti-racist social work, though having such a policy enables you to achieve two things. It gets people who wouldn't normally think about anti-racist social work to do so. And it provides institutional back-up for individuals struggling to get anti-racist social work established in the workplace. Discussions around the adoption of an equal opportunities policy are particularly important in offices which are exclusively or largely white, where the following dictums prevail:

We have no racism operating here.
There are no black workers applying to come to us.
We have no black clients demanding our services.

This is because the debate about whether or not equal opportunities are necessary in their particular situation enables white people to start thinking about racism existing in the absence of black people as well as in their presence, consider how it is reflected in their personal work and in agency policies, and commit themselves to eradicating it. Obtaining the willing and informed consent of white workers at all levels of an organisation is indispensable in ensuring anti-racist social work becomes the norm.

Blockages to equal opportunities

There are a number of dangers bedevilling the efforts of white social workers trying to implement equal opportunities in policy and practice in their agency. One worry is that overt racism will go underground. People will become more subtle and covert in their resistance to racial equality and undermine efforts aimed at securing it. Another is to mistake the implementation of an equal opportunities policy for the establishment of anti-social racial work. This produces situations in which black people are led up the road of false promises where large numbers of black people employed in the lower echelons of the labour hierarchy or a few token blacks sitting on committees are deemed to fulfil equal opportunities policy requirements. I quote one equal opportunities employer who said to me, 'We have our specialist ethnic minorites unit. What more do you want?'

An equal opportunities policy is no more than a tool for endorsing and sustaining other initiatives implementing anti-racist ways of working and establishing egalitarian relations between black and white people. The outcomes of such efforts need to be monitored and evaluated regularly and effectively. The most appropriate people to monitor and evaluate the progress white people make in achieving an agency's anti-racist aims and objectives are black workers and black users of its services organised collectively as a monitoring group. To avoid white people's fears of becoming vulnerable when the racism in their work is revealed from blocking progress on the anti-racist front, white anti-racist social workers and their managers should ensure that a) careful preparatory work is done with these individuals; and b) networks are established to support them in developing their contribution to anti-racist social work. One-to-one counselling which will help them talk through their anxieties and supportive groupwork, coupled with the knowledge that the institution will provide them with the back-up and the retraining they need to ensure they work effectively in an anti-racist environment, are essential in ensuring white resistance does not thwart either personal ambitions in becoming anti-racist or institutional aims and objectives. White anti-racist social workers need their own support networks to help them cope with their fears; release their creativity; share experiences with others; and make demands which are impossible for individuals to take on alone, collectively.

Endorsing an equal opportunities policy requires the commitment of additional resources

Organisations have been declaring themselves equal opportunities employers without releasing the resources necessary for this policy to become a reality. Their initiatives have been restricted to stating that the institution is an 'equal opportunities employer' in advertisements, advertising in the 'ethnic press' and collecting statistics on the ethnic background of applicants for specified jobs. Whilst important advances on previous practice, these moves are inadequate. Advertising in the ethnic press only makes the statement that as an employing authority, the institution is interested in considering applications from groups normally excluded by its normal recruitment procedures. Unless employment practices are transformed to ensure black people are employed at all levels of an organisation in sufficient numbers not to be tokenistic, and under terms and conditions of employment which do not 'dump' the responsibility of dealing with racism in the authority on them, the policy is not worth the cost of printing it.

Employers have to consider recruitment and selection procedures, examining the ways in which applicants are reached; how employees are selected or not for particular jobs; and employment practices once candidates are in post. Recent history is littered with examples of organisations declaring themselves equal opportunities employers, but where black people are found in small numbers, at the lowest rungs of the employment hierarchy, and overworked through the interminable demands made on them (Rooney, 1980). Institutions must find ways through which they can demonstrate that they accept tackling institutional, cultural and individual racism is their responsibility and not that of their black employees. Their employment practices must treat black workers on a par with white ones. This does not mean ghettoising black workers as 'race experts'; forcing them to assume duties which are not contained in their job descriptions; not paying for all their labour; and not promoting them for achieving substantially more than what is required of them (Rooney, 1980; Ohri and Manning, 1982). White organisations and individuals are continually exploiting the knowledge and goodwill of black people who have a vested interest in eradicating racism by asking them to act as teachers whilst keeping them in the role of pupils. White people have devised elaborate structures whereby black people are compelled to work with other black people according to white definitions of the problem. These pathologise black people and strangle the organised resistance they offer racist society (Mullard, 1973). Such mechanisms have created black 'race relations' experts fostering the promotion of black people, largely in the lower levels of the enterprise. These black people are then helped to develop 'good' relationships with their employing agency and elevated to the status of 'community' leaders acceptable to white people for undertaking the task of directly controlling black communities (Mullard, 1973). Fortunately for the future of society, enough black people have resisted this process of incorporation and co-option, highlighting instead the widespread subversion of egalitarian relations between black and white people. What white anti-racist social workers need to do now is to endorse their exposure of the disservice being done to black communities throughout Britain and demand changes in government policy and practice. Central government must foster anti-racist positions actively. The importance of securing central state commitment to anti-racist ways of working has been evidenced in the abolition of the Greater London Council. Many of the GLC's anti-racist initiatives have been discredited through central government action which has subsequently denied these funding to either get off the ground or to consolidate their activities, e.g. the Police Monitoring Committee. Others have been dropped completely with the demise of the GLC. Resistance from the central state can be anticipated because racism is a useful tool for rationing resources. White anti-racist social workers can guard against government opposition by ensuring that their actions are deeply rooted in and strongly supported by the community at large.

Demanding that both local and central state desist from incorporating black activists releases resources which the 'race relations' industry has been 'misusing'. These can be reclaimed and put under the control of people with a black perspective who can use them to make available the services black people need and want. This process can be commenced by altering current policies in relation to the employment of black workers, their recruitment and selection, and the terms and conditions under which they are employed; and by restructuring the Commission on Racial Equality and its attendant organisations so that it changes from being a government-controlled quango into a pressure group under the control of the black population. Forming a lobby, it can define its terms of reference, legislation and programme of action for getting rid of racism in every aspect of public life.

The exploitation of black workers through Section 11 posts

Whilst the commitment to employ more black social workers is being adopted by more local authorities as they become 'Equal Opportunities Employers', many of these appointments are made as Section 11 appointments. Black social workers need to be employed in greater numbers to overcome the effects of previous racist policies undervaluing their practice experience and educational qualifications, and ignoring the disadvantages previously wrought in their lives by racism. But employing black workers primarily through Section 11 contracts reinforces racism in another guise. Posts created under Section 11 of the 1966 Local Government Act are attractive to local authorities because the Home Office guarantees 75 per cent funding for measures reducing discrimination in 'immigrant communities'. Whilst this Act provides one of the few sources of funding specifically targeting racial discrimination, the criticisms against it from an antiracist perspective are legion. To begin with, the framing of this provision, directed at a section of the population being defined as 'the problem', endorses institutionalised racism. It focuses on 'immigrant' communities from the New Commonwealth (later amended to include Pakistan when it left the Commonwealth) which need help in adjusting to the white British way of life. Its aims are assimilationist and rooted in notions of white supremacy – asking black people to become like white people. Their specific needs and experiences can subsequently be ignored because, except for their skin colour, they will have become 'just like us'. Secondly, it assumes that as 'immigrants' black people would not want to retain their culture and own way of life. Desires to the contrary are deemed temporary.

The legislation also contributes to defining black people as 'permanent immigrants' rather than settlers making their own unique contribution to the British way of life. Because black people are not yet accepted as settlers, the children and grandchildren of black people who have emigrated from Third World countries continue to be called 'immigrants' despite their being born in Britain. This perpetuates the idea that black people are temporary residents. White social workers reinforce these definitions when they talk about British-born blacks as 'children of immigrants' – a comment often found in Social Enquiry Reports (SERs). White social workers do not feel compelled to state, 'Jack was the son of

Presbyterian Scottish parents who moved to England in 1981', in their reports to the courts. Thus when they declare that 'Muhammed was the son of Muslim parents who came from Pakistan in 1969', there is an implicit message which they expect white readers of the report to grasp. The message is a racist one which negates black people's contribution to this country and denies their right to be here on the same terms as whites.

The use of Section 11 to provide additional funding for social work posts has been problematic. There have been allegations of the widespread misuse of the monies derived from this particular source of funding (Duffield, 1985; Ely and Denney, 1987). This has resulted in funds intended for specific use in black communities being diverted to general funds, to support activities departments with dwindling resources have been unable to finance from general revenues. These have subsequently cushioned deficits caused by cash-limits, block grants and other cutbacks in public expenditure. This has depoliticised the impact of public expenditure cuts because services which would have otherwise been cut or withdrawn have continued in some fashion. Seeing local authorities struggling to keep services going, white people have kept quiet about declining standards and provisions arising from the cuts. Using Section 11 funding for general purposes, has endangered black organisations by starving them of resources vital to the well-being of black claimants. For example, black self-help groups such as the Asian Resources Centre in Birmingham have been crying out for funds to finance many of their activities for ages, e.g. welfare rights and immigration advice, Asian women's refuges, day care facilities for black elders (Sondhi in Cheetham, 1982; Guru, 1987). Meantime, their local authority has been using Section 11 monies inappropriately (Sharron, 1986). Consequently, black people have been deprived of resources specifically earmarked for them, whilst white people have gained additional funding at their expense. The use of Section 11 funding in these ways is racist. Additionally, as many Section 11 posts have gone to white people, another layer of 'white experts' has been added to those already preventing black people from attending to the needs of black communities in a paid capacity. As one black social worker I interviewed commented:

> I get really upset over the way Section 11 money has been used in this borough. I know that Section 11 money stinks to begin with because it's full of racist ideas. But it was one of the few sources of public money that was to go straight through to black people. But the way it's been used here means that black people were the last ones to see the benefit of it.

Whilst white people employed through Section 11 funding are unnoticed because being white, they can easily be incorporated into the general system, black people are in a different position. Besides being more noticeable, their jobs are often specifically highlighted as Section 11 posts and attached to part of the organisation dealing with 'ethnic minority issues'. Thus black people employed through Section 11 funding are locked onto career ladders with virtually no rungs on them. Jobs secured under this funding are temporary, thereby increasing black people's vulnerability to unemployment. Arrangements for automatically transferring Section 11 funded black people to mainstream career grades are rare. Black people are excluded from a natural progression through to the upper echelons of the labour hierarchy and denied the promotional opportunities open to their white colleagues who are fully employed by local authorities. Thus, whilst Section 11 can be useful in securing a breakthrough for the employment of black workers, it is not good anti-racist practice to stop at this point. Black social workers should be brought into mainstream career structures by being fully employed on the social services payroll immediately. The unions, particularly NALGO, should become involved in securing this piece of organisational change by adopting it as part of the collective bargaining process. In addition, their being locked into specialist units has meant black social workers are required to undertake highly specialised tasks for which they are poorly paid, unless they are employed in an authority which is competing with nearby authorities for their skills. Again, I quote a black social worker who told me:

> I was paid next to nothing until a neighbouring borough offered me a job. Then, all of a sudden I was popular. They were falling over themselves trying to keep me with them. The pay rise which had been a thorn in their flesh for months, suddenly became an open coffer.

Thus, Section 11 posts have provided employers with a means for ghettoising black workers. White anti-racist social workers need to ensure that their organisation's employment policies do not lock black people into Section 11 posts, but move them into mainstream grades with proper opportunities for advancement.

Collective strategies and methods are imperative in implementing organisational change

Initiating organisational change in your agency is a complex task involving the orchestration of action removing individual racism, institutional racism and cultural racism in both policy and practice whilst sustaining the morale of individuals and groups. Individuals can contribute towards organisational change by breaking the conspiracy of silence and speaking out against all instances of racism they detect. It means becoming personally aware of the issues at stake, taking steps to raise consciousness of the matters to be confronted, and facilitating action fostering anti-racist norms. White individuals challenging their organisations also have to seek support for themselves to maintain their morale, sharpen their analysis, work effectively collectively with peers, continually subject their actions to scrutiny, and ensure that their actions do not transgress anti-racist objectives. This requires two forms of organisational change to begin with. The first is that they subject their work to being monitored and evaluated by black people. The second, that they form anti-racist collectives with white people sharing their anti-racist objectives and develop ways of working together. This will be problematic because white people have difficulty accepting an inversion of the normal power relationships between black and white people, including colleagues; and they are more used to competing with each other, even when they allegedly work in teams, than in working collaboratively to benefit one another. Nonetheless, white people will have to work collectively if they are successfully to promote anti-racist policies and practices in spite of the opposition of some white people.

White anti-racist social workers will have to introduce organisational change at all levels of their institutions, including management, other departments in their authority, professional associations and the relevant trade unions. By seeking alliances to underpin campaigns, by direct action and by demanding change among these echelons of their organisation, white anti-racist social workers will strengthen their positions. Without support at these levels, it will be easy for those resisting anti-racist social work to block its implementation. One reason for developing alliances both horizontally and vertically within an organisation is that all aspects of an organisation's policies and practices will be touched by anti-racist changes in one area. People throughout the organisation will be affected. Priorities will have to be re-ordered, competition for resources will be exacerbated, well-known routines will be overturned. Uncertainty and fear of what is being asked of white people will become consonant with strife. In the face of such widespread changes, white people will demand a say in what happens. Without careful preparatory work being undertaken with the individuals concerned, they may well block attempts at altering a racist status quo. They may fear losing the privileges they enjoy and not appreciate the gains that can accrue from working in an anti-racist organisation. For example, implementing an anti-racist curriculum in social work education requires that sociologists, social policy teachers, and psychologists change their teaching content and methods. Whilst white social work educators may see the need for introducing new practices, it may be difficult for them to convince colleagues in other departments of this. Departmental sovereignty, interdepartmental rivalry, professional autonomy, and notions of personal liberty and academic freedom will be used to hinder anti-racist action. The controversy which erupted at Birmingham Polytechnic during the 1986–87 academic year between the social work department and the polytechnic management following the dismissal of a black lecturer is indicative of the difficulties facing a single department embarking on the process of implementing anti-racist social work education (*SWT*, April 1987; Willis, 1987).

Another reason for developing alliances at all levels of an organisation is that it enhances the chances of succeeding in introducing change. Carrying people with you enables them to engage in convincing those who are sceptical about your proposals. Thus the burden of transforming the workplace is spread across a number of shoulders, making it easier for each individual to maintain energy, and enthusiasm for the work. A further reason is that if organisational change is instituted throughout an agency, it becomes more difficult for white people to fob off black colleagues or clients with tokenistic gestures. A collective commitment to anti-racist social work makes it more likely to happen in practice. Demonstrating the reality of anti-racist social work through their practice also allows white people to make a real statement about their commitment to fighting racism. This in turn facilitates the possibility of white people being able to support initiatives developed by black people in ways that do not undermine them, and form alliances based on equality with them.

6

Campaigning for the Transformation of Social Work: the White Social Worker as an Anti-Racist Advocate

The major task of white anti-racist social work advocates is the transformation of existing social work practice and the social relations expressed through and within it. Working in this direction requires white anti-racist social work advocates to break their silence over the destruction racism wreaks on black people's lives. It also demands that they cease acting as 'experts' who can speak for and on behalf of black people. In implementing strategies predicated on fighting racism, white anti-racist social work advocates will have to work simultaneously on the individual or personal level, the institutional or organisational level, and the structural level. This will require white anti-racist social work advocates to work both on their own and collectively to deal with individual distress and structural constraints. The following case studies examine how this work can be done in different contexts – divided families, situations combining sexism with racism, protecting civil liberties and endorsing various forms of kinship.

Under the mounting critique of their work by black activists, white social workers are becoming increasingly aware of the deprivation endured by black people, much of it reinforced through social work intervention perpetuating racism. White social workers can speak out against this state of affairs and bring about change by assuming the role of anti-racist social work advocates. White anti-racist social work advocates would highlight the interconnectedness between the more generalised aspects of institutionalised racism and that occurring within social work, and devote their energies to tackling these simultaneously. White anti-racist social work advocates can engage in organisational change as well as initiate changes in individual practices. Handling this work requires white social workers to adopt an overtly political stance eschewing the 'neutrality' of their position as professionals. For the neutral approach individualises and vacuum-packs social problems, thus making it easy for professionals to pathologise those they are endeavouring to help and hold them solely responsible for their predicament. Through this they collude in maintaining the supremacy of the status quo. In challenging white professionalism, white anti-racist social work advocates begin redefining the social work task and the relations between themselves as employees and their employers, and themselves as workers and service users. Their job is one of constantly highlighting and countering racist policies and practices. Assuming such a position can place white anti-racist social work advocates in an oppositional stance vis-à-vis their white employer, colleagues and service users. In this process, working in anti-racist ways exposes the contradictory relationship between social work's controlling function and its caring one, revealing how social work is used as a tool of oppression, reinforcing control instead of providing for people's welfare. It also highlights the ways in which social work demands the oppressed change themselves by improving their behaviour and adopting more acceptable attitudes; compels them to cope more effectively with their oppression by accepting their predicament as their fault; and ensures that they do not challenge current social relations. The discussion below focuses on how the complex interplay between institutionalised racism and personal suffering can be countered through anti-racist collective action which draws on the energies of white anti-racist social work advocates.

Campaigns against institutionalised racism and its denial of black people's rights

a. Countering the enforced division of black families

White social work advocates have a role in campaigning for black people to have a guaranted right to family life and family forms defined by themselves as the following account illustrates.

A Punjabi Sikh man lost his job in a foundry when he became seriously ill. Although his oldest son aged 15 lived with him in England, his wife and three other children aged 12, 10 and 5 resided in India. He had begun seeking entry certificates for them 15 months earlier, when his health first started deteriorating. His attempts to get compensation from his employers for his illness failed. He was also unsuccessful in getting the DHSS to register him as disabled. His claim for supplementary benefits was allowed only for him and his 15-year-old son, leaving his wife and children in India without any means of support. He went to an Advice Centre for help, but was politely informed by the white workers that none could be provided. The law did not allow him to claim either child benefit or income support in respect of members not resident in Britain.

What could white anti-racist social work advocates do in this case? They would offer the Punjabi Sikh man support in dealing with individual distress, putting him in touch with black organisations with experience in these matters. Moreover, they would ensure that the person was receiving all the benefits to which he and his dependents were entitled, including examining the possibility of lodging appeals against the decisions taken by his former employer and the DHSS. They would also check out whether or not financial support could be provided from other public sources. They would then deal with the institutionalised racism by illiciting the support of relevant MPs and other organisations such as UKIAS and JCWI to pursue the matter further by campaigning to eliminate the racist basis of the immigration and social security laws, linking up with existing campaigns. Many others suffer like this claimant, so that changing the law could alleviate considerable personal suffering amongst a larger group of black people. In trying to secure just and humane legislation, both black and white people would be able to work together. Moreover, in challenging the definition of the law, the process of beginning to transform the nature of social work would be set in train. It would change from what it is – a source of 'help' which colludes with excluding people from receiving justice – to one that gives primacy of place to just treatment for all people.

b. Challenging the distortion of family relationships

White anti-racist social work advocates would also become involved in campaigns endorsing the right of black people to bring their families into Britain by challenging the reinforcement of biological racism through immigration controls emphasising nuclear family relationships and by struggling for the recognition of extended family and other sociological family units. This would include challenging the use of blood tests to prove paternity for black people when paper documentation suffices for others. Asking for proof of *biological* kinship denies that there are other forms of parenting which society can and does recognise, e.g. fostering and adoption. Long-term fostering and adoption of children by others, particularly those who are closely connected with the children's original families, is a common pattern of childcare amongst people from West Africa (Ellis, 1972), the Asian subcontinent and the Caribbean. In the context of only blood ties being accepted as legitimate proof of kinship, many children fostered and adopted by others are deprived of the chance to join their rightful parents.

c. Fighting the combination of sexism and racism

Sexism combines with racism to exacerbate the distress endured by black women. The following cases depict instances in which the social security legislation and its implementation in practice operates to the detriment of black women's welfare:

> After living in England several years, Shama's marriage broke down because her husband physically abused her and her daughter aged 3. She sought safety in a white women's refuge because there were no facilities nearby specifically earmarked for Asian women. Her claim for supplementary benefit was rejected because she could not produce her passport. It was being held by her husband who said he would give it to her when she returned home.

Besides exposing the racism evident in the demand that Shama produce her passport to establish her residence in Britain rather than taking her word for it as happens for white people, this case reveals the sexism underpinning the social security system. Shama cannot prove her claim to social security because she is dependent on her husband and does not have her own passport. White anti-racist social work advocates can become involved in campaigns abolishing the requirement that black people produce passports in order to have access to resources when in need, and demanding women's right to an independent income.

The white anti-racist social work advocate would respond to Shama's personal distress by helping her find a place in an Asian women's refuge by driving her to one; and supporting her claim for supplementary benefit, passing the case on to a black organisation when the issues to be addressed are more complicated than advice giving. Having done this, white anti-racist social work advocates would address institutionalised racism. Becoming involved in campaigns directed at securing resources for autonomous refuges for black women and the employment of black workers in centres allegedly catering for the needs of all women who come through their doors, would constitute part of the struggle against that.

Finally, they would back campaigns insisting on women's right to resources responding to their specific needs, e.g. housing.

d. Campaigning for an anti-racist social security system

The British income maintenance system caters primarily for the needs of white British people. Its provisions are based on norms that are consistent with reinforcing class rule by maintaining the work ethic (Ginsburg, 1978), reproducing gender oppression by treating women as dependent on men and having similar working patterns to them (Pascall, 1985); and perpetuating racial oppression (Gordon, 1985). Those elements within the social security system which comprise institutionalised racism include: disallowing child benefit for people living in Britain if their children reside overseas, even though this may be the result of immigration laws preventing their entry (Gordon, 1985); denying supplementary benefit to sponsored dependents (CCAB, 1983); and refusing family income supplement and unemployment benefit to dependents living overseas when the person providing their main source of income support resides in Britain (Gordon, 1985). The changes introduced in the income maintenance system following the Fowler Review will intensify institutionalised racism through the 'residence test' and demands for passports to establish eligibility for those who 'appear foreign' (LSSC, 1986). Social workers will become more extensively involved in its application through their role in the Social Fund.

Other changes in black people's position have resulted from linking immigration status with income maintenance entitlements. The 1980 Social Security Act has made the liability of sponsors to maintain their dependents legally enforceable and failure to do so can constitute a criminal offence. Consequently, people who subsequently become unemployed and registered as such, are unable to claim income support for sponsored dependents. This puts black families under enormous financial pressure in times of hardship because the sponsoring family's money will have to be stretched to cover the needs of the sponsored family. The net effect of this will be further to impoverish and divide black families.

Other aspects of the social security legislation which need changing cover a range of additional categories denied access to the system despite demonstrable hardship and suffering. These are 'overstayers'; 'overseas' students' and 'illegal immigrants'. Black people, particularly refugees, can be classified as 'overstayers' simply if they are in Britain whilst the Home Office processes their application (Gordon and Newnham, 1985). Regulations concerning deportation orders prohibit black people from applying for supplementary benefit if they are appealing such an order (D'Orey, 1984). Overseas students cannot claim either housing or supplementary benefits, although they may receive urgent needs payments for limited periods, if their funds have been delayed, e.g. by postal failure, or coups in their countries of origin. 'Illegal immigrants' are excluded from access to public income maintenance provisions. The term 'illegal immigrant' is especially contentious, for it has become very broadly defined, to include people who have withheld information from immigration officers, unintentionally as in the case of *Zamir* heard in the House of Lords in 1980, though this possibility was rejected when the House of Lords adjudicated on the case of *Khawaja* in 1982, and those whose information the immigration officer does not believe, including documentary evidence such as birth and marriage certificates (CRE, 1985). These expanded definitions of illegality have undermined the position of legally settled black people. Police 'fishing raids', justified under the banner of seeking 'illegal immigrants', jeopardise the civil liberties of black people whose home is Britain, and amplify the racist view that they do not *'really belong here'*. White anti-racist social work advocates can be involved in campaigns affirming the rights of black people to be in Britain as full citizens, regardless of their length of stay. An anti-racist social security system would grant rights to all people living and working here by virtue of that fact alone. Simply living and working in Britain and being in need would constitute the eligibility requirement. The 'overseas' dependents of people living and working in Britain would automatically be covered under its provisions.

e. Protecting civil liberties through campaigns

Parveen Khan's situation reflects the position black people face when thinking they are legally settled in Britain, their status is officially undermined (Gordon and Newnham, 1985). The continuous expansion of the definition of 'illegal immigrant' in the hands of the Home Office, the police, and the courts, makes the outcome of struggles aimed at ensuring justice in particular circumstances difficult to predict.

> Parveen Khan was declared an illegal immigrant when her husband, who had come to Britain when 13, was found to have done so as the son of a sociological rather than biological parent. When threatened with deportation, her husband went into hiding, and Parveen Khan went to claim supplementary benefit. However, despite the *Khawaja* ruling, Parveen was considered an 'illegal immigrant' and her claim was refused. Her child benefit for her British born child was also withdrawn. A campaign was launched to prevent her removal from Britain and to raise money for her support. As a result of this campaign, Parveen Khan was able to remain (Gordon and Newnham, 1985).

> A further example of a campaign safeguarding a black person's right to work in this country and provide a service to black people was that concerning Mohamed Idris, a social worker threatened with deportation when asking for an extension to his visa. A lengthy campaign mounted in his defence rallied NALGO as well as black and white social workers to his cause. Mohamed Idris was ultimately allowed to stay.

White anti-racist social work advocates can join campaigns resisting encroachment on the civil liberties of black people and participate actively in campaigning organisations such as the Action Group on Immigration and Nationality (AGIN).

They can support individuals experiencing immigration difficulties by putting them in touch with others in a similar predicament and with black people who have specific expertise on these issues. On the organisational front, white anti-racist social workers can join campaigns aimed at changing the law in directions which secure the civil liberties of black people, e.g. prohibiting fishing raids.

White anti-racist social work advocates concerned with ensuring justice in the situations described above can become involved in campaigns which demand:

1. the cessation of the arrest without warrant of those suspected of being illegal immigrants;
2. allegations of 'illegal immigration' status be proved by the Home Office and the police;
3. immigration laws which assume people are innocent until proved guilty rather than the reverse;
4. the humane treatment of immigration detainees;
5. the elimination of the racism inherent in the immigration laws, nationality laws, and the remainder of the legal system;
6. the elimination of the racism inherent in the prison system; police service, probation service, and personal social services;
7. the cessation of treating black people as 'immigrants' simply because of the colour of their skin;
8. the recognition of the gamut of black family forms; and
9. the safeguarding of black women's rights both within the family and outside it.

Joining campaigns outside mainstream social work will enable white anti-racist social work advocates to make connections between enhancing black people's welfare and making demands for better personal social services for other client groups.

Anti-racist social work practice is good practice

The cases considered above demonstrate that white anti-racist social work advocates have a role in highlighting gaps in provisions and the failure of services to meet black people's needs. They can argue that black people are damaged by inappropriate intervention on the part of white social workers, e.g. the destruction of black children's identity as a result of transracial adoption, the unjust penalising of black youth in the juvenile justice system, the exclusion of black people from the benefits of the income maintenance system, thereby drawing parallels between anti-racist social work and good practice generally. White anti-racist social work advocates would also devote their energies towards bringing black and white people together on the basis of equality, using their commitment to anti-racist ways of working in building a bridge leading white people to the formation of a non-racist social work. Thus they can add to the celebration of a common struggle through the recognition of equality in diversity described by black women as 'Many Voices, One Chant' (*Feminist Review*, 1984).

White anti-racist social work advocates can challenge bad practice on a more general level, e.g. the absence of interpreting facilities. Currently, the lack of either sufficient bilingual social workers or appropriate translation services has led to bad practice on a wide scale across settings. For example, social services use children to translate for their elders, and the probation service uses volunteer interpreters without adequate training, pay or understanding of the work they are undertaking. White anti-racist social work advocates can also work to attract resources for oppressed groups and support black people's demands for resources, power and autonomy. Their work reveals the necessity of introducing different techniques and methodologies into mainstream social work. Their relationships with service users would be characterised by equality and an expertise geared towards servicing individuals and groups defining for themselves the provisions they need. The major aim of the professional–claimant relationship based on servicing consumers would be to provide individuals and groups with the information and back-up support required in achieving their goals. White anti-racist social work advocates would also constantly ask the question, '*What are the implications of what I am doing for black people?*', so as not to decontextualise race or ignore the significance of racism in their behaviour, thought or actions. In becoming anti-racist social work advocates, white social workers would have to lose their stereotypes of black individuals and communities and acquire detailed knowledge about the existence of resources which could be marshalled in favour of deprived communities, black and white. Focusing on putting *justice* back into their work, white anti-racist social work advocates seek to empower powerless groups acting for themselves. The business of empowering others puts them in the position of *listeners* responding to the voice of service users. The oppressed have their own voice and can and do speak for themselves. But their voices are seldom heard in a bureaucracy taking its own goals and objectives as the definitive ones when making decisions about people's lives. So white anti-racist social work advocates would be listening to voices which are already there to be heard. Their activities thus reveal the necessity of introducing different techniques and methodologies into mainstream social work. Community action approaches, with their campaigning, networking and collective ways of working, become essential tools for white anti-racist social work advocates.

Bringing community action approaches, with their emphasis on collective ways of working, into maintsream social work facilitates recognition of the connection between an individual's position, their personal suffering and the structural factors impinging on their lives. Looking at the situation in these terms enables white anti-racist social work advocates to put meaning into the statement that the 'personal is political' and acknowledge that individual woes reflect their social status. In using community action tools and tactics, white anti-racist social work advocates would contribute towards exposing the real nature of the problems to be tackled and redefining these by focusing on the racist nature of society; organising with others collectively to introduce structural change; and using political analyses and action in responding to personal needs. By giving them real control and choice over what to do with their lives, structural change becomes essential in liberating individuals. Structural change also promotes the welfare of all people – black and white.

The links between anti-racist struggles and poverty more generally have to be highlighted and incorporated in the action plans of white anti-racist social work advocates. This means dealing with white working-class clients' racism, particularly in inner-city areas so that they can build bridges between black and white communities and focus on the commonality of their struggle. These bridges cannot be constructed on the assumption that class oppression has precedence over race, but on recognising the multiple aspects of oppression black people have to endure. Nor can these bridges be built on pious hopes and abstract words. They have to have a concrete reality which demystifies relationships between black and white communities.

Tackling racism means getting the discussion going on the right tracks. As long as 'positive discrimination' is popularly construed as giving oppressed groups 'something they do not deserve', talking about 'positive discrimination' for black people will not attract many deprived white people to fighting racism. Such terminology confirms white racist stereotypes of the inferiority of black people and prepares the ground for the white backlash, as the American experience is demonstrating. 'Positive discrimination' defined in these terms makes the relationship between black and white people one of recipient and donor respectively and reproduces paternalism. Moreover, it mystifies the real problem that needs to be addressed. This is that black people as a group are not receiving their entitlements, and that their present experience and qualifications are being ignored (Smith, 1976; Brown, 1984). The 'positive discrimination' approach disguises the fact that a real redistribution of resources from one group to another requires the transferral of resources on three levels simultaneously – from the wealthy to the poor, i.e. between classes, from men to women, and from white to black. 'Positive discrimination' also negates the position of black people as they experience it. In not acknowledging black people's view of being denied access to power and resources and being deprived of common justice, *'positive discrimination' is denying black people their voice and making invisible their experience of racism.*

Thus, white anti-racist social work advocates need to talk about *equalising action securing justice for black people.* Equalising action is aimed at redistributing social power and resources towards black people so that they receive their share of society's power and wealth and gain full recognition of the qualities they already possess. In demystifying the nature of the social relations inherent in policies of 'positive discrimination', white anti-racist social work advocates will complement the work of others similarly involved in exposing the real nature of the social relations underpinning racist situations and enable both black and white people to see the commonality of their struggle against racism.

White anti-racist social work advocates would highlight the purpose of their struggle as righting the past and present injustices meted out to black people and increasing resources to everyone in deprived communities through immediate action aimed at an egalitarian transformation of the system whereby wealth and power are distributed. Such an approach offers white anti-racist social work advocates a stronger basis for united action between blacks and whites and overcomes the divisiveness which is a central feature in the dynamics of racism. Their activities must also link up with anti-racist struggles being carried out more generally in society.

Engaging in anti-racist ways of working enables white anti-racist social work advocates to examine the specific ways in which class, race and gender oppress different groups of people. White anti-racist social work advocates struggle against all social divisions, e.g. race, class, gender, disability, sexual orientation and age, because these are used to both control people and ration resources between them. Oppression can occur along any number of dimensions. Oppression on the basis of class, race, gender, disability, age and sexual orientation is central to our present society which is permeated by relations of domination and subordination. Individuals experiencing oppression through a number of these dimensions experience them simultaneously, not one by one. Thus oppression operates on the principle of accretion rather than accumulation. The anti-racist struggle is a struggle for equality for all people regardless of their status in society. But to foster a common struggle between black and white people against class or any other form of oppression, alliances must be constructed on foundations which explicitly acknowledge the different starting points between people, the significance of such differences in their life chances and developing their particular strengths, differences in the power relations between them as well as the similarities in their experience of oppression more generally (Lorde, 1984). White anti-racist social work advocates must not prioritise one form of oppression over another, thereby creating a new hierarcy of oppression in the organisations they create to eliminate it. Moreover, in making connections between one dimension of oppression, e.g. race, and another, e.g. gender or class, white anti-racist social work advocates must ensure that they do not use these as diversions taking attention away from the business of tackling racial oppression. At the same time, they must take care not to conclude that the specificity of one form of oppression can be subsumed by another.

White anti-racist social work advocates should become involved in a number of campaigns, challenging the racist bases of social work and its provisions. These include: campaigning against the racist immigration rules which divide black families and cause untold sorrow and hardship (Gordon, 1986; CRE, 1985); arguing for the proper funding of social services for black people instead of their relegation to Section 11 provisions; demanding resources especially earmarked for black women (Guru, 1987) and black elders (ASRA, 1981); reversing racist stereotypes and images of black individuals, families and communities; and demanding the elimination of racist conditions in social security provisions, housing, education, health and employment. Campaigning in these areas is important for enhancing the conditions underpinning the quality of life and welfare of black people. Provisions coming through the personal social services can augment the quality of black people's lives, they cannot substitute for it. But provisions in the personal social

7

Conclusions: Developing Anti-Racist/Non-Racist Social Work

Racist social work education and practice have been unchallenged for far too long. The glaring injustice these perpetuate and the damage they cause to black people and ourselves can no longer be ignored. White people have no choice but to become anti-racist if they wish to reclaim their humanity and live in a society worth having. That is, a society in which justice, caring, individual fulfilment and collective concern reign. Anti-racist social work has a role to play in creating a non-racist society. Fulfilling this role calls for the transformation of social work and demands that its own practice espouses equality for all; fosters consumer involvement; develops provisions for meeting people's needs rather than for rationing resources; endorses a professionalism based on caring for people not controlling them. The implementation of these demands requires the employment of workers who have demonstrated an ability to work with anyone, across racial divides, client groups and sexes, and who have an empathy based on knowledge of the differences between black and white people and their significance rather than the pretense that people are all the same. This requires a change in the fundamental basis of social work and the redefinition of its task. It means asserting the values of being human in a context lacking notions of racial superiority, but in which respect, dignity and value are accorded to all. It is also not about one set of individuals or groups gaining at the expense of others. Competition between people would give way to collaboration. Egalitarian working relations would replace hierarchical ones.

161

Anti-racist social work

Anti-racist social work has got to introduce change at both personal and institutional levels. Individual conduct in interpersonal relations and the allocation of power and resources in society have got to be transformed if racism is to be eliminated. To get anti-racist social work firmly implanted in Britain, white people must:

1. change the current definition of the social work task to one which does not render oppression invisible;
2. negate the 'objectivity' currently imbedded in a professionalism underpinning a status quo which has been found seriously wanting;
3. alter the existing power relationship between the users of services and workers. The voice of the 'expert' should not substitute for that of the oppressed;
4. not deny consumers their right to determine the types of welfare provisions on offer;
5. stop treating people's welfare at both individual and group level as a commodity that can be rationed for the purposes of controlling people and their aspirations. Instead, it should enhance personal fulfilment and well-being;
6. change the basis of training which assumes a false neutrality on the major social and ethical issues of the day to one making explicit its value base and taking a moral and political stance against oppression in any of its forms;
7. terminate an allocation of power and resources perpetuating injustice and misery and replace it with one committed to implementing justice and equality for all;
8. ending the theoretical separation between social work and a) other key elements of the state, especially welfare sectors, e.g. housing, education, health and society security; and b) the 'law and order' apparatus including the police and the courts, the Home Office, and the Immigration Service. Instead, the connections between each of these parts must be made visible;

9. end the separation between policy and practice, exposing the connections between them; and

10. replacing the lack of political commitment to end racial inequality, with one operating in the opposite direction.

From the variety of changes that are envisaged, it is clear that not only will anti-racist social work end racism, but it will expose and tackle other forms of oppression which are reproduced by and perpetuated through social work too. In particular, changes eradicating class and gender inequality will be included in the transformation resulting from the struggle against racism. Because of its impact on other forms of oppression, anti-racist social work will signal the implementation of good social work practice all round. In addition, tackling racism aimed at black people undermines the racist practices perpetrated against other non-Anglo-Saxon ethnic minorities.

Having adopted and developed an anti-racist position in social work, white social workers will have to move on to developing non-racist social work. This will have to be done in conjunction with black social workers, on the basis of equality in relationships between the two. This means equal power, equal access to resources, equal opportunities and prospects, and work that is equal in value. Ultimately, the development of non-racist social work will mean that both black and white social workers will work across the whole range of client groups. But the nature of their work will have been transformed. Their main emphasis will not be on rationing resources, but on using them effectively, collectively, in providing people with the services they require when they need them. This in turn will require that these are underpinned by egalitarianism and involve consumers fully in determining the nature of service provision and delivery. Such services will have to be funded through the public purse. Thus, to secure non-racist social work, black and white social workers will have to change the political, juridical and social basis of current practice. When this has taken place, anti-racist social work will provide the foundation for achieving equality and transforming welfare provisions for

both black and white people. Social work, redefined according to anti-racist criteria, is not about social control, but about realising significant improvements in the life chances and well-being of individuals, regardless of their gender, race, class, age, physical or intellectual abilities, sexual orientation, religious affiliation, or linguistic capabilities. Anti-racist social work, therefore, is a bridge between social work in a racist society and social work in a non-racist one.

Useful Addresses

All Faiths for One Race (AFFOR)
1 Finch Road
Lozells
Birmingham B19 1HS

Manchester Law Centre
595 Stockport Road
Longsight
Manchester

Commission for Racial Equality (CRE)
Elliot House
10–12 Allington Street
London SW1E 5EH

Joint Council for the Welfare of Immigrants (JCWI)
44 Theobalds Road
London WC1X 8SP

The Runnymede Trust
37A Grays Inn Road
London WC1X 8PP

United Kingdom Immigrants Advisory Service (UKIAS)
Brettenham House
7th Floor
Savoy Street
Strand
LondonWC2 7EN

Action Group on Immigration and Nationality (AGIN)
44 Theobalds Road
London WC1X 8SP

Migrants' Action Group
68 Charlton Street
London NW1

Black and In Care Steering Group
c/o Children's Legal Centre
20 Compton Terrace
London N1 2UN

The White Collective for Anti-Racist Social Work
c/o The Department of Applied Social Studies
The University of Warwick
Coventry CV4 7AL

The New Black Families Unit
121–123 Camberwell Road
Lewisham
London SE17

The Mickleton Group
c/o Jenny Read
Student Unit Supervisor
The Albany Centre
Douglas Way
Deptford
London SE8

Bibliography

Association of British Adoption and Fostering Agencies (ABAFA) (1977) *Soul Kids Campaign Report*, London, ABAFA.

Adamson, M. and Borgos, S. (1985) *The Mighty Dream: Protest Movements in the United States*, London, Routledge.

Age Concern (1984) *Housing for Ethnic Elders*, London, Age Concern.

Ahmed, S. (1978) 'Asian Girls and Cultural Conflicts' in *Social Work Today*, August.

Ahmed, S. (1982) 'Social Work with Minority Children and Families', Unit 16 in *Ethnic Minorities and Community Relations*, Open University Course No. E354, Milton Keynes, OU.

Ahmed, S. (1984) 'Social Work with Ethnic Minorities', paper given at the BASW Annual Conference at Nene College, April.

Ahmed, S., Cheetham, J. and Small, J. (1987) *Social Work with Black Children and Their Families*, London, Batsford.

All London Teachers Against Racism and Fascism (1984) *Challenging Racism*, London, ALTARF.

Amos, V. and Parmar, P. (1984) 'Challenging Imperial Feminism' in *Feminist Review*, no. 17, Autumn.

Asian Sheltered Residential Accommodation (1981) *Asians Sheltered Residential Accommodation*, London, ASRA.

Association of Black Social Workers and Allied Professionals (1981) *Black Children in Care: Evidence Submitted to the Select Committee on Child Care*, London, ABSWAP.

Association of Directors of Social Services and Commission for Racial Equality (1978) *Multi-Racial Britain: The Social Services Response*, London, ADSS/CRE.

Arnold, E. (1982) 'Finding Black Families for Black Children' in *Social Work and Ethnicity*, ed. J. Cheetham, London, Allen & Unwin.

Bagley, C. and Young, L. (1982) 'Policy Dilemmas and the Adoption of Black Children' in *Social Work and Ethnicity*, ed. J. Cheetham, London, Allen & Unwin.

Bailey, R. and Brake, M. (1975) *Radical Social Work*, London, Edward Arnold.

167

Banks, G. (1971) 'The Effects of Race on One-to-One Helping Interviews' in *Social Service Review*, vol. 45, June, pp. 137–46.

Barker, M (1981) *The New Racism: Conservatives and the Ideology of the Tribe*, London, Junction Books.

Ben-Tovim, G. and Gabriel, J. (1982) 'The Society of Race: Time to Change Course?' in A. Ohri *et al.* (eds) *Community Work and Racism*, London, Routledge.

Beresford, P. and Croft, S. (1986) *Whose Welfare: Private Care or Public Services*, Brighton, Lewis Cohen Urban Studies Centre.

Bhalla, A. and Blakemore, K. (1981) *Elders of the Ethnic Minority Groups*, Birmingham, All Faiths for One Race.

Billingsley, A. and Giovannoni, J. (1972) *Children of the Dream*, New York, Harcourt Brace Jovanovich.

Black and In Care Steering Group (1984) *Black and in Care: Conference Report*, London, Blackrose Press.

Blom-Cooper, L. (1986) *A Child in Trust: The Report of the Panel of Inquiry into the Circumstances Surrounding the Death of Jasmine Beckford*, London Borough of Brent, Kingswood Press.

Bolger, S., Corrigan, R., Docking, J. and Frost, N. (1981) *Towards Socialist Welfare Work*, London, Macmillan.

Brent Community Health Council (1981) *Black People and the Health Service*, Brent, Brent CHC.

Brinton, L. and Welch, M. (1983) 'White Agency, Black Community' in *Adoption and Fostering*, 7(2), pp. 16–18.

Brittan, A. and Maynard, M. (1984) *Sexism, Racism and Oppression*, Oxford, Blackwell.

Bromley, D. and Longino, C. F., Jnr. (1972) *White Racism and Black Americans*, Cambridge, Mass., Schenkman.

Brook, E. and Davis, A. (1985) *Women, The Family and Social Work*, London, Tavistock.

Brown, B. (1986) 'Adding the "Cream" Weakens' in *Social Work Today*, 7 July, p. 7.

Brown, C. (1984) *Black and White Britain: The Third PSI Survey*, London, Heinemann.

Bryan, B., Dadzie, S. and Scafe, S. (1985) *The Herat of the Race: Black Women's Lives in Britain*, London, Virago.

Butrym, Z. (1968) *Medical Social Work in Action*, London, Bell.

Carby, H. (1982) 'White Woman Listen! Black Feminism and the Boundaries of Sisterhood' in Centre for Contemporary and Cultural Studies, *The Empire Strikes Back*, London, Hutchinson.

Carmichael, S. (1971), *Soul on Ice*, New York, Panther.

Cashmore, E. (1979) *Rastaman*, London, Allen & Unwin.

Cashmore, E. and Troyna, B. (eds) (1982) *Black Youth in Crisis*, London, Allen & Unwin.

Castles, S. and Kosack, G. (1972) 'The Function of Labour Immigration in Western European Capitalism' in *New Left Review*, 73, May/June, pp. 8–21.

Central Council for Education and Training in Social Work (1978) *Social Work Training and Ethnic Minorities*, London, CCETSW.

Central Council for Education and Training in Social Work (1985) *Ethnic Minorities and Social Work Training*, Paper 21.1, London, CCETSW.

Centre for Contemporary and Cultural Studies (1982) *The Empire Strikes Back: Race and Racism in 1970s Britain*, London, Hutchinson.

Chapeltown Citizens Advice Bureau (1983) *Immigrants and the Welfare State*, London, Blackrose Press.

Cheetham, J. (1972) *Social Work with Immigrants*, London, Routledge.

Cheetham, J. (1982) *Social Work Services for Ethnic Minorities in Britain and the USA*, London, DHSS.

Cheetham, J. (ed.) (1982) *Social Work and Ethnicity*, London, Allen & Unwin.

Chestang, L. (1972) 'The Dilemma of Bi-Racial Adoption' in *Social Work*, May, pp. 102.

Coard, B. (1971) *How West Indian Children are made Educationally Subnormal*, London, New Beacon.

Cohen, P. (1986) *The Perversions of Inheritance*, unpublished paper from the Institute of Education, London.

Cohen, S. (1981) *The Thin End of the White Wedge: The New Nationality Laws – Second Class Citizenship and the Welfare State*, Manchester, Manchester Law Centre.

Comer, J. P. and Poussaint, A. P. (1975) *Black Child Care*, New York, Pocket Books.

Commission for Racial Equality (1977) *A Home from Home? Some Policy Considerations on Black Children in Residential Care*, London, CRE.

Commission for Racial Equality (1979) *Barlavington Manor Children's Home: Report of a Formal Investigation*, London, CRE.

Commission for Racial Equality (1984) *Hackney Housing Investigated: Summary of a Formal Investigation Report*, London, CRE.

Commission for Racial Equality (1985) *Immigration Control Procedures: Report of a Formal Investigation*, London, CRE.

Community Relations Commission (1976a) *Between Two Cultures: A Study of Relationships Between Generations in the Asian Community in Britain*, London, CRC.

Community Relations Commission (1976b) *Working in Multi–Racial Areas: A Training Handbook for Social Services Departments*, London CRC.

Coombe, V. and Little, A. (1986) *Race and Social Work: A Guide to Training*, London, Tavistock.

Compton, B. and Galaway B. (1975) *Social Work Processes*, Homewood, Ill., The Dorsey Press.

Corrigan, P. (1977) 'The Welfare State and Class Struggle' in *Marxism Today*, March.

Corrigan P. and Leonard, P. (1979) *Social Work Under Capitalism*, London, Macmillan.

Counter Information Services (1978) *Racism*, London, CIS.

Coventry Evening Telegraph (1987) 'Homes Call Needs More Study', 4 June, p. 2.

Cox, O. (1970) *Caste, Class and Race*, New York, Monthly Review Press.

Cowell, T., Jones, T. and Young, J. (1982) *Policing the Riots*, London, Junction Books.

Curno, P. (ed.) (1978) *Political Issues in Community Work*, London, Routledge.

Davis, A. (1981) *Women, Race and Class*, London, The Women's Press.

Davis, A. (1987) *A Class Approach to the Struggle Against Racism*, lecture given in Hackney Race Relations Unit Celebrations for International Women's Week.

Denney, D. (1983) 'Some Dominant Perspectives in the Literature Relating to Multi-Racial Social Work' in *British Journal of Social Work*, 13(2), pp. 149–74.

Devine, D. (1983) 'Defective, Hypocritical and Patronising Research' in *Caribbean Times*, 4 March, p. 4.

Devine, D. (1985) *Submission to the Beckford Inquiry*, June.

Devine, D. (1986) 'Fostering Getting' in *West Indian Digest*, no. 134, October, pp. 10–15.

Dominelli, L. (1978a) 'The Welfare State and the Public Expenditure Cuts' in *Bulletin of Social Policy*, no. 1, Spring.

Dominelli, L (1978b) 'Racism' in *Bulletin of Social Policy*, no. 2, Summer.

Dominelli, L (1979) 'The Challenge for Social Work Education' in *Social Work Today* 10(25), pp. 27–9.

Dominelli, L. (1982) *Community Action: Organising Marginalised Groups*, Reykjavik, Kwenna Frambothid.

Dominelli, L. (1983) *Women in Focus: Community Service Orders and Female Offenders*, Warwick University, Nuffield Foundation Research Report.

Dominelli, L. (1984) *Working with Families: A Feminist Perspective*, paper delivered at BASW Annual Conference, Nene College, April.

Dominelli, L. (1986) 'Father–Daughter Incest: Patriarchy's Shameful Secret' in *Critical Social Policy*, 16, Spring, pp. 8–22.

Dominelli, L. (1987) Speech at Anti-Racist Social Work Conference at Sheffield University, 6–9 April.

Dominelli, L. and McLeod, E. (1982) 'The Personal and the A-Political: Feminism and Moving Beyond the Integrated Methods Approach' in R. Bailey and P. Lee (eds) *Theory and Practice in Social Work*, Oxford, Blackwell, pp. 112–27.

Duffield, M. (1985) *Social Work Today*, April.

D'Orey, S. (1984) *Immigration Prisoners: A Forgotten Minority*, London, Runnymede Trust.

Ebony (1986) *Special issue on the black family*, August.

Eichler, M. (1984) *Families in Canada Today: Recent Changes and Policy Consequences*, Toronto, Gage.

Ellis, J. (1972) 'The Fostering of West African Children in England' in J.

Triseliotis (ed.) *Social Work with Coloured Immigrants and Their Families*, London, Institute of Race Relations/Oxford University Press.

Ely, P. and Denny, D. (1987) *Social Work in a Multi-Racial Society*, Aldershot, Gower.

Emecheta, B. (1983) *Adah's Story*, London, Allison and Busby.

Eysenck, A. R. (1971) *Race, Intelligence and Education*, Aldershot, Temple Smith.

Fanon, F. (1968) *Black Skins, White Masks*, London, MacGibbon & Kee.

Farrah, M. (1986) *Black Elders in Leicester*, Leicester, Leicester Social Services Department Report.

Fitzherbert, J. (1967) *West Indian Children in London*, London, Bell.

Fletchman-Smith, B. (1984) 'Effects of Race on Adoption and Fostering' in *International Journal of Social Pshyciatry*, vol. 30, pp. 121–8.

Foner, N. (1979) *Jamaica Farewell*, London, Routledge.

Foot, P. (1965) *Immigration and Race in British Politics*, Harmondsworth, Penguin.

Foren, R. and Batta, I. (1970) 'Colour as a Variable in the Use Made of a Local Authority Child Care Department' in *Social Work Today*, 27(3), pp. 10–15.

Fox, L. (1982) 'The Value Position in Recent Child Care Law and Practice' in *British Journal of Social Work*, 12(3), pp. 265–90.

Freire, P. (1970) *The Pedagogy of the Oppressed*, Harmondsworth, Penguin.

Fryer, P. (1984) *Staying Power: The History of Black People in Britain*, London, Pluto.

Genovese, E. (1974) *Roll Jordon Roll: The World the Slaves Made*, New York, Pantheon.

Gifford, Lord (1986) *The Broadwater Farm Inquiry*, London Borough of Haringey.

Gilder, G. (1982) *Wealth and Poverty*, London, Buchan & Enright.

Gill, O. and Jackson, B. *Black Children in White Families: Transracial Adoption in Britain*, London, Batsford.

Gilroy, P. (1980) 'Managing the Underclass: A Further Note on the Sociology of Race Relations in Britain' in *Race and Class*, 22(1), pp. 47–62.

Gilroy, P. (1982a) 'Police and Thieves' in Centre for Contemporary and Cultural Studies, *The Empire Strikes Back*, London, Hutchinson.

Gilroy, P. (1982b) 'You Can't Fool the Youths: Race and Class Formation in the 1980s' in *Race and Class*, 23(2/3), pp. 207–22.

Gilroy, P. (1987) *There Ain't No Black in the Union Jack*, London, Hutchinson.

Ginsburg, N. (1979) *Class, Capital and Social Policy*, London, Macmillan.

Gitterman, A. and Schaeffer, A. (1972) 'The White Professional and the Black Client' in *Social Casework*, May, pp. 280–91.

Gobineau, J. A. (1953) *Essai Sur L'Inégalité des Races Humaines*, Paris, Firmin and Didot, 4th edn, repr. in 1960s.

Gordon, P. (1981) *Passport Raids and Checks Britain's Internal Immigra-*

tion Controls, London, Runnymede Trust.

Gordon, P. (1984) *White Law: Racism in the Police, Courts and Prisons*, London, Pluto.

Gordon, P. (1985) *Policing Immigration: Britain's Internal Controls*, London, Pluto.

Gordon, P. (1986) 'Racism and Social Security' in *Critical Social Policy*, 17, Autumn.

Gordon, P. and Newnham, A. (1985) *Passport to Benefits: Racism in Social Security*, London, Child Poverty Action Group and the Runnymede Trust.

Greater London Council (1984) *Anti-Racist Trade Union Working Group Report*, London.

Gulbenkian Community Work Group (1973) *Current Issues in Community Work*, London, Gulbenkian (Calouste) Foundation.

Gurnah, A. (1984) 'The Politics of Racism Awareness Training' in *Critical Social Policy*, Winter.

Guru, S. (1987) 'An Asian Women's Refuge' in S. Ahmed *et al.* (eds), *Social Work with Black Children and Their Families*, London, Batsford.

Gutman, H. (1976) *The Black Family in Slavery and Freedom: 1925–1970*, New York, Vintage.

Hall, S. (1980a) 'Race, Articulation and Societies Structured in Dominance' in UNESCO (ed.), *Sociological Theories: Race and Colonialism*, pp. 305–45.

Hall, S. (1980b) 'Popular Democratic Versus Authoritarian Populist: Two Ways of Taking Democracy Seriously' in Hunt (ed.), *Marxism and Democracy*, pp. 157–87.

Hall, S. *et al.* (1978) *Policing the Crisis: Mugging, The State and Law and Order*, London, Macmillan.

Hartmann, P. and Husband, C. (1974) *Racism and the Media*, London, Davis-Poynter.

Hearn, J. (1982) 'Radical Social Work: Contradictions, Limitations and Political Possibilities' in *Critical Social Policy*, 2(1), pp. 19–34.

Hill, R. (1972) 'The Strengths of Black Families' in D. Bromley *et al.* (ed.), *White Racism and Black Americans*, Cambridge, Mass., Schenkman.

Hiro, D. (1971) *Black British, White British*, New York, Monthly Review Press.

Holland, B. and Lewando-Hundt, G. (1986) *The Ethnic Minority Elderly Survey: Method, Data and Applied Action*, Coventry Social Services Department, Ethnic Minorities Development Unit.

Home Office (1986) *Ethnic Minorities, Crime and Policing*, London, HMSO.

Hooks, B. (1981) *Ain't I A Woman: Black Women and Feminism*, London, Pluto.

Husband, C. (1980a) 'Culture, Context and Practice: Racism in Social Work' in Bailey, R. and Brake, M. (eds), *Radical Social Work*, pp. 64–85.

Husband, C. (1980b) 'Notes on Racism in Social Work Practice' in *Multi-Racial Social Work*, no. 1, 5–15.

Husband, C. (1982) *Race, Identity and British Society*, Open University course E354 Units 5 and 6, Milton Keynes, OU.

Husband, C. (1986) 'Racism, Prejudice and Social Policy' in V. Coombe and A. Little (eds), *Race and Social Work,* London, Tavistock, pp. 3–13.

Hutchinson-Reis, M. (1986) 'After the Uprising – Social work on the Broadwater Estate' in *Critical Social Policy*, no. 17, Autumn, pp. 70–80.

Jacob, S. (1985) 'Race, Empire and the Welfare State: Council Housing and Racism' in *Critical Social Policy*, no. 13, Summer.

Jansari, A. (1980) 'Social Work with Ethnic Minorities: A Review of the Literature' in *Multi-Racial Social Work*, no. 1, pp. 17–34.

Jenson, A. R. (1972) *Genetics and Education*, London, Methuen.

John, G. (1978) *Black People*, Milton Keynes, Open University, Unit 23.

Jones, C. (1977) *Immigration and Social Policy in Britain*, London, Tavistock.

Jones, C. (1983) *State Social Work and the Working Class*, London, Macmillan.

Kadushin, L. (1972) 'The Racial Factor in the Interview' in *Social Work*, May, pp. 173–89.

Katz, J. (1978) *White Awareness*, University of Oklahoma Press.

Kent, B (1972) 'The Social Worker's Cultural Pattern as it affects Casework with Immigrants' in J. Triseliots (ed.), *Social Work With Coloured Immigrants and Their Families*, London, Institute for Race Relations/Oxford University Press, pp. 38–54.

Khan, V. (ed.) (1979) *Support and Stress: Minority Families in Britain*, London, Macmillan.

King, M. and May, C. (1985) *Black Magistrates*, London, The Cobden Trust.

Lambeth Social Services Committee (1981) *Black Children in Care Report*, London, Lambeth SSD.

Lawrence, E. (1982a) 'Just Plain Common Sense: The Roots of Racism' in Centre for Contemporary and Cultural Studies, *The Empire Strikes Back*, London, Hutchinson, pp. 47–94.

Lawrence, E. (1982b) 'In the Abundance of Water the Fool is Thirsty' in Centre for Contemporary and Cultural Studies, *The Empire Strikes Back*, London, Hutchinson, pp. 95–142.

Lawrence, J. (1983) 'Should White Families Adopt Black Children' in *New Society*, 30 June, pp. 499–501.

Layton-Henry, Z. (1985) *The Politics of Race in Britain*, London, Allen & Unwin.

Lea, J (1980) 'The Condradictions of the Sixties Race Relations Legislation' in *Permissiveness and Control*, National Deviancy Conference, London, Macmillan, pp.122–48.

Leeds Social Security Campaign (1986) *The Response to the Fowler Review and the 1986 Social Security Act*, Leeds, LSSC.

Lees, R. and McGrath, M. (1975) 'Community Work with Immigrants' in *British Journal of Social Work*, 4(2), pp. 175–86.

174   *Bibliography*

Littlewood, R. and Lipsedge, M. (1982) *The Aliens and the Alienists: Ethnic Minorities and Psychiatry*, Harmondsworth, Penguin.
Loney, M. (1986a) *The Politics of Greed: The New Right and the Welfare State*, London, Pluto.
Loney, M. (1986b) 'Imagery and Reality in the Broadwater Farm Riot' in *Critical Social Policy*, 17, Autumn, pp. 81–6.
Lorde, A.(1984) *Sister Outsider*, New York, The Crossing Press.
McCulloch, J. and Kornreich, R. (1974) 'Black People and the Social Services Departments: Problems and Perspectives' in M. Brown (ed.), *Social Issues and the Social Services*, London, Charles Knight, pp. 145–76.
Malek, F. (1985) *Asian Women and Mental Health or Mental Ill Health: The Myth of Mental Illness*, Southwark, Asian Women's Aid.
Mama, A. (1984) 'Black Women, the Economic Crisis and the British State' in *Feminist Review*, no. 17, Autumn, pp. 19–36.
Manning, B. and Ohri, A. (1982) 'Racism: the Response of Cummunity Work', in Ohri, A. *et al.* (eds) *Community Work and Racism*, London, Routledge, pp. 3–23.
Marchant, H. and Wearing, B. (1986) *Gender Reclaimed*, Hale and Iremonger.
Miles, R. (1982) *Capitalism, Racism and Migrant Labour*, London, Routledge.
Miles, R. (1987) 'Recent Marxist Theories of Nationalism and the Issue of Racism' in *British Journal of Sociology*, 38(1), pp. 24–43.
Milner, D. (1975) *Children and Race*, Harmondsworth, Penguin.
Milner, D. (1983) *Children and Race – Ten Years On*, Harmondsworth, Penguin.
Minford, P. (1984) 'State Expenditure: A Study in Waste' in *Economic Affairs*, April–June, pp. 79–90.
Mizio, E. (1972) 'White Worker – Minority Client' in *Social Work*, May.
Moore, R. (1975) *Racism and Black Resistance in Britain*, London, Pluto.
Morrison, T. (1986) *The Bluest Eye*, London, Triad/Grafton Books.
Moynihan, D. P. (1965) *The Negro Family: The Case for National Action*, Washington DC, US Department of Labor.
Mullard, C. (1973) *Black Britain*, London, Allen & Unwin.
Mullender, A. and Miller, D. (1985) 'The Ebony Group: Black Children in White Foster Homes' in *Adoption and Fostering*, vol. 9, no. 1, pp. 33–49.
Network 21: A Newsletter to Promote an Anti-Racist Perspective in Social Work Education and Training (1986) Edinburgh, Moray House College of Education, October.
Oakley, A. (1972) *Sex, Gender and Society*, London, Temple Smith.
Ohri, A., Manning, B. and Curno, P. (1982) *Community Work and Racism*, London, Routledge.
Orphanides, K. (1986) 'The Cypriot Community in Britain; in V. Coombe and A. Little (eds), *Race and Social Work*, London, Tavistock, pp. 80–87.
Ousley, H. (1981) *The System*, London, Runnymede Trust.

Ousley, H. (1983) *Ethnic Minorities and Social Services – Children in Care*, London, Greater London Council.

Panton, D. (1986) 'Educating the Whites' in *Social Work Today*, 21 July, p. 6.

Parmar, P (1982) 'Gender, Race and Class: Asian Women in Resistance' in Centre for Contemporary Culture Studies, *The Empire Strikes Back*, London, Hutchinson, pp. 236–75.

Pascall, G. (1986) *Social Policy: A Feminist Analysis*, London, Tavistock.

Pennie, P. and Williams, W. (1987) 'Black Children Need the Richness of Black Family Life' in *Social Work Today*, 2 February, p. 12.

Phillips, M. (1982) 'Separatism or Black Control' in A. Ohri and B. Manning (eds.), *Community Work and Racism*, London, Routledge, pp. 103–120.

Philp, M. (1979) 'Notes on the Form of Knowledge in Social Work' in *The Sociological Review*, 27(1), pp. 83–111.

Pincus, A. and Minahan, A. (1973) *Social Work Practice: Model and Method*, Itasca, Ill., F. E. Peacock Publishers, Inc.

Pinder, R. (1984) *Probation Work in a Multi-Racial Society*, unpublished paper, University of Leeds.

Plummer, J. (1978) *Divide and Deprive*, London, Joint Council for the Welfare of Immigrants.

Pollert, A. (1985) *Unequal Opportunities: Racial Discrimination and the Youth Training Scheme*, Birmingham, TURC Publishing.

Powell, D. and Edmonds, J. (1985) 'Are You Racist Too?' in *Community Care*, 14 September.

Prescod-Roberts, M. and Steele, N. (1980) *Black Women: Bringing it All Back Home*, Bristol, Falling Wall Press.

Pryce, K. (1979) *Endless Pressure: A Study of West Indian Life-Styles in Bristol*, Harmondsworth, Penguin.

Rainwater, L. (1972) 'Crucible of Identity: The Negro Lower Class Family' in D. Bromley and C.F. Longino Jnr (eds), *White Racism and Black Americans*, Cambridge, Mass., Schenkman.

Raynor, L. (1970) *Adoption of Non-White Children: The Experience of a British Adoption Project*, London, Allen & Unwin.

Reeve, A. and Stubbs, P. (1981) 'Racism and the Mass Media: Revising Old Perspectives' in *Multi-Racial Education*, 9(2), pp. 41–55.

Reeves, J. F. (1983) *British Racial Discourse*, Cambridge University Press.

Rex, J. (1981) 'Errol Lawrence and the Sociology of Race Relations: An Open Letter' in *Multi-Racial Education*, 10(1), pp. 49–51.

Rex, J. and Moore, R. (1967) *Race, Community and Conflict: A Study of Sparkbrook*, London, Institute of Race Relations/Oxford University Press.

Rex, J. and Tomlinson, S. (1979) *Colonial Immigrants in a British City: A Class Analysis*, London, Routledge.

Rhamdanie, B. (1978) *Handsworth Alternative Scheme*, A Project undertaken under the auspices of the (West Midlands) Birmingham Probation Service.

Riley, J. (1985) *The Unbelonging*, London, The Women's Press.

Rooney, B. (1980) 'Active Mistakes – A Grass Roots Report' in *Multi-Racial Social Work*, no. 1, pp. 43–54.

Rooney, B. (1982) 'Black Social Workers in White Departments' in J. Cheetham (ed.) *Social Work and Ethnicity*, pp. 184–96.

Rose, E. (1968) *Colour and Citizenship*, London, Oxford University Press/Institute of Race Relations.

Rowe, J. and Lambert, L. (1973) *Children Who Wait*, London, Association of British Adoption Agencies.

Ruben, G. (1975) 'The Traffic in Women' in R. Reiter (ed.), *Toward an Anthropology of Women*, New York, Monthly Review press, pp. 165–9.

Ryan, W. (1972) 'Savage Discovery: The Moynihan Report' in D. Bromley and C. F. Longino Jnr (eds), *White Racism and Black Americans*, Cambridge, Mass., Schenkman.

Satymurti, C. (1981) *Occupational Survival*, Oxford, Blackwell.

Seebohm, Lord (1968) *Report of the Committee on Local Authority and Allied Personal Social Services,* London, HMSO.

Segal, L. (ed.) (1983) *What's To Be Done About The Family?*, Harmondsworth, Penguin.

Sewell, T. (1985) 'The Black Child in Danger' in *The Voice*, 7 September, p. 14.

Simpkin, M. (1980) *Trapped Within Welfare: Surviving Social Work*, London, Macmillan.

Sharron, H. (1985) 'Rob the Poor – Give to the Rich' in *Social Work Today*, vol. 16, no. 27, pp. 6–7.

Sivanandan, A. (1983) 'Challenging Racism: Strategies for the 80s' in *Race and Class* 25(2), pp. 1–11.

Sivanandan, A. (1985) 'RAT and the Degradation of Black Struggle' in *Race and Class*, 26(4), pp. 1–33.

Sivanandan, A. (1976) 'Race, Class and the State: the Black Experience in Britain' in *Race and Class*, 17(4), pp. 437–68.

Small, J. (1984) 'The Crisis in Adoption' in *International Journal of Psychiatry*, vol. 30, Spring, pp. 129–41.

Small, J. (1987) 'Transracial Placements: Conflicts and Contradictions' in S. Ahmed *et al.* (eds), *Social Work with Black Children and Their Families*, London, Batsford.

Smith, D. (1976) *The Facts of Racial Disadvantage: PEP Report*, Harmondsworth, Penguin.

Solomos, J. *et al.* (1982) 'The Organic Crisis of British Capitalism and Race: The Experience of the Seventies', in Centre for Contemporary and Cultural Studies, *The Empire Strikes Back*, London, Hutchinson, pp. 9–46.

Solomos, J. (1986) 'Varieties of Marxist Conceptions of "Race", Class and the State, A Critical Analysis' in J. Rex and Mason (eds), *Theories of Race and Ethnic Relations*, Cambridge, Cambridge University Press, pp. 49–78.

Sondhi, R. (1982) 'The Asian Resources Centre' in J. Cheetham (ed.), *Ethnicity and Social Work*, London, Oxford University Press, pp. 165–74.

Spender, D. (1980) *Man Made Language*, London, Routledge.

Statham, D. (1978) *Radicals in Social Work*, London, Routledge.

Stone, M. (1981) *The Education of the Black Child in Britain: The Myth of Multiracial Education*, London, Fontana.

Stubbs, P. (1985) 'The Employment of Black Social Workers: From "Ethnic Sensitivity" to Anti-Racism' in *Critical Social Policy*, 12, Spring, pp. 6–27.

Stubbs, P. (1987) 'Racism and the Left' in *Critical Social Policy*, 20, Autumn, pp. 91–7.

Stubbs, P. (1987) 'Professionalism and the Adoption of Black Children' in *British Journal of Social Work*, vol. 17, no. 5, pp. 473–92.

Taylor, W. (1981) *Probation and After-Care in a Multi-Racial Society*, London, Commission on Racial Equality.

Thorburn, J. (1986) *Permanence in Child Care*, Oxford, Blackwell.

Tipler, J. (1986) *Is Justice Colour Blind? A Study of the Impact of Race in the Juvenile Justice System in Hackney*, Hackney Social Services Department Resarch Paper, no. 6.

Tizard, B. (1977) *Adoption, A Second Chance*, London, Open Books.

Tower Hamlets Tenants Federation (1986) *Tenants Tackling Racism*, Stepney, Dame Colet House.

Triseliotis, J. (ed.) (1972a) *Social Work with Coloured Immigrants and Their Families*, London, Institute of Race Relations/Oxford University Press.

Triseliotis, J. (1972b) 'The Implications of Cultural Factors in Social Work With Immigrants' in J. Triseliotis (ed.), *Social Work with Coloured Immigrants and Their Families*, London, Institute of Race Relations/Oxford University Press.

Weare, P. (1986) 'Why Dan and Oliver Can Deal with Racism' in *Social Work Today*, 28 July, p. 9.

White, E. (1984) 'Listening to the Voices of Black Feminism' in *Radical America*, 18(2/3), pp. 7–12.

Whitehouse, P. (1986) 'Race and the Criminal Justice System' in V. Coombe and A. Little (eds), *Race and Social Work*, London, Tavistock, pp. 113–25.

Williams, F. (1987) 'Racism and the Discipline of Social Policy: A Critique of Welfare Theory' in *Critical Social Policy*, September.

Willis, P. (1977) *Learning to Labour: How Working Class Kids Get Working Class Jobs*, Aldershot, Gower.

Wilson, A. (1978) *Finding a Voice*, London, Virago.

Wilson, E. (1977) *Women and the Welfare State*, London, Tavistock.

Wood, C. (1974) 'Life Styles Among West Indians and Social Work Problems' in *New Community*, 3(3), pp. 249–54.

Wright, R. (1968) *Native Son*, Harmondsworth, Penguin.

Index